PRISM
READING

Student's Book

3

Alan S. Kennedy
Chris Sowton

with
Christina Cavage

CAMBRIDGE
UNIVERSITY PRESS

CAMBRIDGE
UNIVERSITY PRESS

University Printing House, Cambridge CB2 8BS, United Kingdom

One Liberty Plaza, 20th Floor, New York, NY 10006, USA

477 Williamstown Road, Port Melbourne, VIC 3207, Australia

314–321, 3rd Floor, Plot 3, Splendor Forum, Jasola District Centre, New Delhi – 110025, India

79 Anson Road, #06–04/06, Singapore 079906

Cambridge University Press is part of the University of Cambridge.

It furthers the University's mission by disseminating knowledge in the pursuit of education, learning and research at the highest international levels of excellence.

www.cambridge.org
Information on this title: www.cambridge.org/9781108601146

First published 2018

20 19 18 17 16 15 14 13 12 11 10 9 8 7 6 5 4 3 2 1

Printed in Malaysia by Vivar

A catalogue record for this publication is available from the British Library

ISBN 978-1-108-60114-6 Prism Reading 3 Student's Book with Online Workbook
ISBN 978-1-108-45534-3 Prism Reading 3 Teacher's Manual

CONTENTS

SCOPE AND SEQUENCE

UNIT	READING PASSAGES	KEY READING SKILLS	ADDITIONAL READING SKILLS
1 GLOBALIZATION *Academic Disciplines* Cultural Studies / Sociology	1 Turkish Treats (blog post) 2 Changing Eating Habits in Italy (essay)	Making predictions from a text type Scanning topic sentences Taking notes on supporting examples	Understanding key vocabulary Annotating Reading for details Working out meaning Making inferences Reading for main ideas Paraphrasing Identifying purpose and audience Synthesizing
2 EDUCATION *Academic Disciplines* Communications / Education	1 Should I Major in Business or Engineering? (article) 2 Distance vs. Face-to- Face Learning (article)	Making inferences Using a Venn diagram	Understanding key vocabulary Using your knowledge Reading for main ideas Reading for details Taking notes Synthesizing
3 MEDICINE *Academic Disciplines* Health Sciences / Medicine	1 The Homeopathy Debate (debate) 2 Should Healthcare Be Free? (blog post)	Annotating a text	Understanding key vocabulary Using your knowledge Previewing Reading for details Identifying opinions Skimming Reading for main ideas Scanning to find key words Making inferences Synthesizing
4 THE ENVIRONMENT *Academic Disciplines* Ecology / Environmental studies	1 Controlling Certain Disaster (interview) 2 Combatting Drought in Rural Africa (report)	Identifying cohesive devices	Understanding key vocabulary Predicting content using visuals Reading for details Making inferences Using your knowledge Reading for main ideas Taking notes Synthesizing

LANGUAGE DEVELOPMENT	WATCH AND LISTEN	SPECIAL FEATURES
Academic alternatives to phrasal verbs Globalization vocabulary	Chinese Flavors for American Snacks	Critical Thinking Collaboration
Education vocabulary Academic words	College Debt and Bankruptcy	Critical Thinking Collaboration
Medical vocabulary Academic vocabulary	A New Way to Handle Allergies	Critical Thinking Collaboration
Academic noun phrases Natural disaster vocabulary	Population and Water	Critical Thinking Collaboration

UNIT	READING PASSAGES	KEY READING SKILLS	ADDITIONAL READING SKILLS
5 ARCHITECTURE *Academic Disciplines* Architecture / Urban Planning	1 We Need More Green Buildings (article) 2 Form, Function, or Both? (essay)	Skimming a text	Using your knowledge Understanding key vocabulary Reading for details Annotating Making inferences Summarizing Understanding paraphrase Synthesizing
6 ENERGY *Academic Disciplines* Engineering / Physics	1 Renewable Energy (fact sheet) 2 Reduce, Reuse, Recycle (essay)	Working out meaning from context	Predicting content using visuals Understanding key vocabulary Reading for main ideas Reading for details Using your knowledge Taking notes Making inferences Synthesizing
7 ART AND DESIGN *Academic Disciplines* Design / Fine Art	1 All that Art Is (article) 2 Photography as Art (essay)	Scanning to find information	Understanding key vocabulary Predicting content using visuals Reading for details Taking notes Making inferences Using your knowledge Reading for main ideas Understanding paraphrase Identifying opinions Synthesizing
8 AGING *Academic Disciplines* Economics / Sociology	1 The Social and Economic Impact of Aging (interview) 2 Saudi Arabia: The Realities of a Young Society (case study)	Using your knowledge to predict content	Understanding key vocabulary Reading for details Making inferences Taking notes on main ideas Scanning to find information Working out meaning Synthesizing

LANGUAGE DEVELOPMENT	WATCH AND LISTEN	SPECIAL FEATURES
Academic word families Architecture and planning vocabulary	Building a Green Home	Critical Thinking Collaboration
Energy collocations Formal and informal academic verbs	Wind Turbines	Critical Thinking Collaboration
Paraphrasing Vocabulary for art and design	A Culinary Art Canvas	Critical Thinking Collaboration
Academic collocations with prepositions Language of prediction	Senior Exercise	Critical Thinking Collaboration

① READING

Receptive, language, and analytical skills
Students improve their reading skills through a sequence of proven activities. First they study key vocabulary to prepare for each reading and to develop academic reading skills. Then they work on synthesis exercises in the second reading that prepare students for college classrooms. Language Development sections teach vocabulary, collocations, and language structure.

READING 1

PREPARING TO READ

1 UNDERSTANDING KEY VOCABULARY Read the definitions. Complete the sentences with the correct form of the words in bold.

aesthetic (adj)	relating to the enjoyment or study of beauty, or showing great beauty
conceptual (adj)	based on ideas or principles
contemporary (adj)	existing or happening now
distinction (n)	a difference between similar things
established (adj)	generally accepted or familiar; having a long history
notion (n)	a belief or idea
significance (n)	importance

1 A sculpture in which the artist's main idea or message is considered more important than the technique can be called _____ art.

2 The new museum in town has a lot of _____ appeal. The exterior of the building is very beautifully designed.

3 It is common these days to prefer _____ architecture, but I like the classic, old homes in my neighborhood.

4 In art class we learned the _____ between fine art and applied art.

5 It is now well _____ that Pablo Picasso was one of the great artists of the twentieth century.

6 Art historians often explain the _____ of very famous works of art and how they may have influenced our society.

7 Many people share the _____ that the term "art" also applies to things like car and video game design.

ALL THAT ART IS

❶ **What is art?** This question has puzzled philosophers and great thinkers for centuries. In fact, there is disagreement about exactly what art is. Most of us would agree that Leonardo da Vinci's Mona Lisa is art, but what about a video game? One dictionary definition states that art is "making objects, images, or music, etc. that are beautiful or that express certain feelings." This, however, could be regarded as too broad a definition. There are actually a number of different categories of objects and processes under the umbrella term of art that can be explored.

❷ Art is typically divided into two areas: fine art (such as painting, sculpture, music, and poetry) and applied art (such as pottery, weaving, metalworking, furniture making, and calligraphy). However, some claim that the art label can also be attached to car design, fashion, photography, cooking, or even sports. Fine art is categorized as something that only has an **aesthetic** or **conceptual** function. This point was made over a thousand years ago by the Greek philosopher Aristotle, who wrote, "the aim of art is to represent not the outward appearance of things but their inward **significance**." He noted that artists produced objects, drama, and music that reflected their emotions and ideas, rather than just trying to capture a true image of nature. Andy Warhol, the American artist famous for his Pop Art in the 1960s, once said, "An artist produces things that people don't need to have." This is the **distinction** between fine and applied art. Applied arts require an object to be functional as well as beautiful.

❸ In the twentieth century, artists began to challenge the **established** idea of art. They recognized that their work belonged to the higher social classes who had the wealth to purchase art and the leisure time to enjoy it. The architect Frank Lloyd Wright commented, "Art for art's sake is a philosophy of the well-fed." In an attempt to challenge this **notion**, the French painter Marcel Duchamp submitted a toilet to an art exhibition in 1917 instead of a painting. He signed it and said, "Everything an artist produces is art." Today, many people complain about the lack of skill in the production of conceptual artistic objects. Some **contemporary** artists use assistants to produce all their art for them. British artist Damien Hirst claims that as long as he had the idea, it is his work. He has compared his art to architecture, saying, "You have to look at it as if the artist is an architect, and we don't have a problem that great architects don't actually build the houses."

> ❝ **Everything an artist produces is art.** ❞

❹ Despite a hundred years of modern art, fine art is still regarded as a preserve of the wealthy. Hirst's works, for example, sell for millions of dollars. Even so, we can see examples of art all around us that are not expensive. Many towns and cities have public art that can be enjoyed by all. Some museums, like the National Gallery of Art in Washington, D.C., are free. Others are free for children and students. Street art is also popular in different neighborhoods around the world. One British artist, Banksy, has become world-famous for unauthorized[1] works of art painted on building walls. These can be viewed at no charge by anyone who knows where to look.

❺ Art anthropologist Ellen Dissanayake, in the book *What is Art For?* offers one intriguing function of art: "the heightening of existence." In other words, art makes our ordinary, everyday lives a little more special. This notion may not apply to all art, but perhaps we can agree that it is a good goal toward which all artists should reach.

[1]**unauthorized** (adj) without official permission

126

127

2 MORE READING

Critical thinking and collaboration

Multiple critical thinking activities prepare students for exercises that focus on academic reading skills. Collaboration activities help develop higher-level thinking skills, oral communication, and understanding of different opinions. By working with others students, they become better prepared for real life social and academic situations.

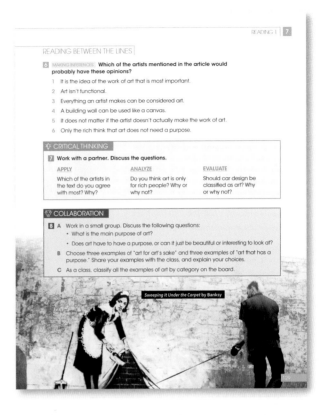

READING 1   7

READING BETWEEN THE LINES

6 MAKING INFERENCES **Which of the artists mentioned in the article would probably have these opinions?**

1 It is the idea of the work of art that is most important.
2 Art isn't functional.
3 Everything an artist makes can be considered art.
4 A building wall can be used like a canvas.
5 It does not matter if the artist doesn't actually make the work of art.
6 Only the rich think that art does not need a purpose.

☼ CRITICAL THINKING

7 **Work with a partner. Discuss the questions.**

APPLY	ANALYZE	EVALUATE
Which of the artists in the text do you agree with most? Why?	Do you think art is only for rich people? Why or why not?	Should car design be classified as art? Why or why not?

⚘ COLLABORATION

8 A Work in a small group. Discuss the following questions:
  • What is the main purpose of art?
  • Does art have to have a purpose, or can it just be beautiful or interesting to look at?

  B Choose three examples of "art for art's sake" and three examples of "art that has a purpose." Share your examples with the class, and explain your choices.

  C As a class, classify all the examples of art by category on the board.

Sweeping It Under the Carpet by Banksy

3 VIDEO

Summarizing the unit

Each unit ends with a carefully selected video clip that piques student interest and pulls together what they have learned. Video lessons also develop key skills such as prediction, comprehension, and discussion.

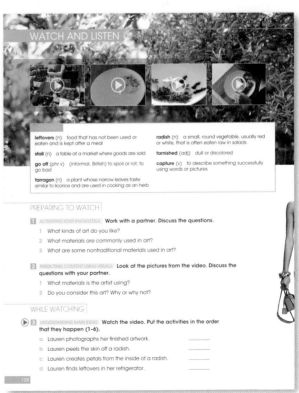

WATCH AND LISTEN

leftovers (n)   food that has not been used or eaten and is kept after a meal

stall (n)   a table at a market where goods are sold

go off (phr v)   (informal, British) to spoil or rot; to go bad

tarragon (n)   a plant whose narrow leaves taste similar to licorice and are used in cooking as an herb

radish (n)   a small, round vegetable, usually red or white, that is often eaten raw in salads

tarnished (adj)   dull or discolored

capture (v)   to describe something successfully using words or pictures

PREPARING TO WATCH

1 ACTIVATING YOUR KNOWLEDGE **Work with a partner. Discuss the questions.**

1 What kinds of art do you like?
2 What materials are commonly used in art?
3 What are some nontraditional materials used in art?

2 PREDICTING CONTENT USING VISUALS **Look at the pictures from the video. Discuss the questions with your partner.**

1 What materials is the artist using?
2 Do you consider this art? Why or why not?

WHILE WATCHING

3 UNDERSTANDING MAIN IDEAS **Watch the video. Put the activities in the order that they happen (1–6).**

a Lauren photographs her finished artwork.   _____
b Lauren peels the skin off a radish.   _____
c Lauren creates petals from the inside of a radish.   _____
d Lauren finds leftovers in her refrigerator.   _____

138

Capturing interest

- Students experience the topics and expand their vocabulary through captivating readings and videos that pull together everything they have learned in the unit, while developing academic reading and critical thinking skills.

- Teachers can deliver effective and engaging lessons using Presentation Plus.

Building confidence

- *Prism Reading* teaches skills that enable students to read, understand, and analyze university texts with confidence.

- Readings from a variety of academic disciplines in different formats (essays, articles, websites, etc.) expose and prepare students to comprehend real-life text they may face in or outside the classroom.

Extended learning

- The Online Workbook has one extra reading and additional practice for each unit. Automated feedback gives autonomy to students while allowing teachers to spend less time grading and more time teaching.

Research-based

- Topics, vocabulary, academic and critical thinking skills to build students' confidence and prepare them for college courses were shaped by conversations with teachers at over 500 institutions.

- Carefully selected vocabulary students need to be successful in college are based on the General Service List, the Academic Word List, and the Cambridge English Corpus.

PATH TO
BETTER LEARNING

CLEAR LEARNING OBJECTIVES

Every unit begins with clear learning objectives.

RICH CONTENT

Highly visual unit openers with discussion questions are engaging opportunities for previewing unit themes.

SCAFFOLDED INSTRUCTION

Activities and tasks support the development of critical thinking skills.

COLLABORATIVE GROUP WORK

Critical thinking is followed by collaborative tasks and activities for the opportunity to apply new skills. Tasks are project-based and require teamwork, research, and presentation. These projects are similar to ones in an academic program.

CRITICAL THINKING

After reading, targeted questions help develop critical thinking skills. The questions range in complexity to prepare students for higher-level course work.

EXTENDED LEARNING OPPORTUNITIES

In-class projects and online activities extend learning beyond the textbook.

BETTER
LEARNING

BLOOM'S TAXONOMY

Prism Reading prepares students for college coursework by explicitly teaching a full range of critical thinking skills. Critical thinking exercises appear in every unit of every level, organized according to the taxonomy developed by Benjamin Bloom.

Critical thinking exercises are highlighted in a special box and indicates which skills the students are learning.

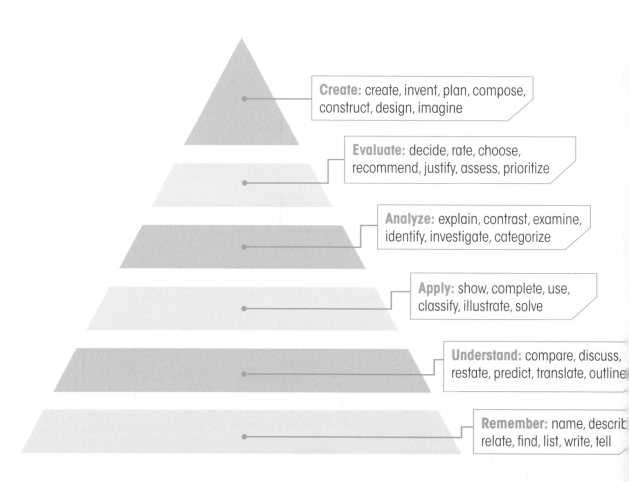

⚙ CRITICAL THINKING

7 SYNTHESIZING **Work with a partner. Use ideas from Reading 1 and Reading 2 to discuss the questions.**

APPLY
Have you ever taken an artistic photograph? Describe it.

APPLY
Do you agree with the author's thesis "It cannot be said that photography is unquestionably art"?

ANALYZE
Can a photograph really be worth $4.5 million? Why or why not?

Create: create, invent, plan, compose, construct, design, imagine

Evaluate: decide, rate, choose, recommend, justify, assess, prioritize

Analyze: explain, contrast, examine, identify, investigate, categorize

Apply: show, complete, use, classify, illustrate, solve

Understand: compare, discuss, restate, predict, translate, outline

Remember: name, describ[e] relate, find, list, write, tell

HIGHER-ORDER THINKING SKILLS

Create, Evaluate, Analyze

Students' academic success depends on their ability to derive knowledge from collected data, make educated judgments, and deliver insightful presentations. *Prism Reading* helps students gain these skills with activities that teach them the best solution to a problem, and develop arguments for a discussion or presentation.

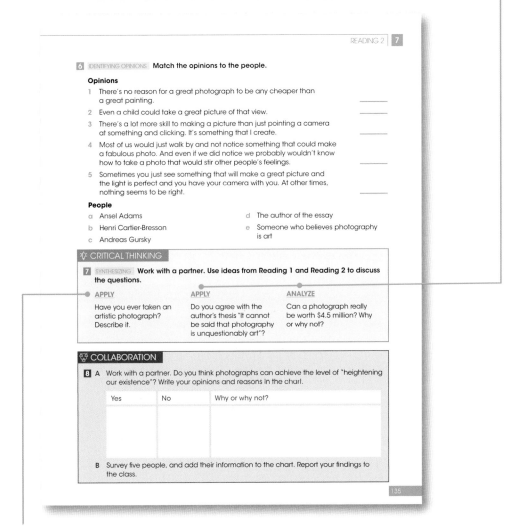

READING 2 | 7

6 IDENTIFYING OPINIONS **Match the opinions to the people.**

Opinions

1 There's no reason for a great photograph to be any cheaper than a great painting. _____

2 Even a child could take a great picture of that view. _____

3 There's a lot more skill to making a picture than just pointing a camera at something and clicking. It's something that I create. _____

4 Most of us would just walk by and not notice something that could make a fabulous photo. And even if we did notice we probably wouldn't know how to take a photo that would stir other people's feelings. _____

5 Sometimes you just see something that will make a great picture and the light is perfect and you have your camera with you. At other times, nothing seems to be right. _____

People

a Ansel Adams

b Henri Cartier-Bresson

c Andreas Gursky

d The author of the essay

e Someone who believes photography is art

CRITICAL THINKING

7 SYNTHESIZING **Work with a partner. Use ideas from Reading 1 and Reading 2 to discuss the questions.**

APPLY

Have you ever taken an artistic photograph? Describe it.

APPLY

Do you agree with the author's thesis "It cannot be said that photography is unquestionably art"?

ANALYZE

Can a photograph really be worth $4.5 million? Why or why not?

COLLABORATION

8 A Work with a partner. Do you think photographs can achieve the level of "heightening our existence"? Write your opinions and reasons in the chart.

Yes	No	Why or why not?

B Survey five people, and add their information to the chart. Report your findings to the class.

135

LOWER-ORDER THINKING SKILLS

Apply, Understand, Remember

Students need to be able to recall information, comprehend it, and see its use in new contexts. These skills form the foundation for all higher-order thinking, and *Prism Reading* develops them through exercises that teach note-taking, comprehension, and the ability to distill information from charts.

GLOBALIZATION

ACTIVATE YOUR KNOWLEDGE

Work with a partner. Discuss the questions.

1   What types of food are made in your country and sold in others? Do you buy food and other products from other countries?

2   Does it matter that people now import so many goods from other countries? Why or why not?

3   What effects has globalization had on your country?

PREPARING TO READ

1 UNDERSTANDING KEY VOCABULARY **Read the sentences and write the words in bold next to the definitions.**

1 A food critic wrote that she was impressed by the sushi restaurant's **authenticity** and how it is run by chefs from Japan.

2 The chef at this restaurant is well known for being a **perfectionist**. He takes a long time to prepare his dishes, and he will not serve them unless they look exactly right.

3 The fish at this restaurant is always extremely **fresh**. If it has been in the kitchen for more than one day, they will not use it.

4 The restaurant is **situated** near the river, which is a very popular place.

5 The food critic **insists** that people must visit the restaurant.

6 The restaurant is offering a **discount**: anyone who eats dinner before 7:00 p.m. on Monday only has to pay 50% of the menu prices.

7 Besides the delicious food, according to the critic, another **selling point** of the restaurant is that it has beautiful, traditional Japanese furniture and art on the walls.

8 Good chefs use the best **ingredients** when they cook to make sure the food is flavorful and delicious.

a _____ (adj) recently made, collected, or cooked

b _____ (n) a feature that persuades people to buy a product

c _____ (n) a reduction in the usual price

d _____ (n) food that is used with other foods in the preparation of a particular dish

e _____ (n) a person who wants everything to be perfect and demands the highest standards possible

f _____ (adj) in a particular place

g _____ (v) to say firmly or demand forcefully

h _____ (n) the quality of being real or true

⚒ SKILLS

MAKING PREDICTIONS FROM A TEXT TYPE

Different text types, such as essays, articles, and blogs, have different characteristics. Some will be more suitable for academic study than others. Before reading a text, you can make predictions about the information and the style of the writing. The source, title, and any pictures can help you predict the content.

2 PREDICTING CONTENT **You are going to read a blog post. Before reading, which of the statements do you think will be true?**

1 The style will be informal.

2 The contents will be appropriate for an academic essay.

3 The writer will give his or her personal opinions.

4 The information will be up-to-date.

Shinjuku's Omoide Yokocho is a popular eating area in Tokyo, Japan.

TURKISH TREATS

More information

FOLLOWERS
201k

ELSEWHERE

1 Hello Minneapolis foodies!

MODA IN EAST CALHOUN

2 I'm kicking off this week's blog by talking about a fantastic new Turkish restaurant in East Calhoun called Moda. I can't remember ever eating better Turkish food—it was so delicious! In fact, this is one of the things that the restaurant prides itself on[1]—the **fresh ingredients** and **authenticity** of the cooking. Apparently, the chef insists that the fruit and vegetables be brought over twice a week from his home region in Turkey—and from nowhere else. He may be a **perfectionist**, but it was so delicious that I can't complain. Moda isn't cheap, but it's definitely worth every penny.

3 And I have great news for you. When I told him that I write a food blog, he said he'd give all my readers a 10% **discount**! Just mention this blog when you make a reservation.

CHEZ FITZ DOWNTOWN

4 A very different restaurant, where I had lunch last Monday, is Chez Fitz. **Situated** near downtown, its main **selling point** is that its food is all locally sourced[2] within 20 miles (32 kilometers) of the restaurant. My friends and I were completely amazed—we had no idea that so much could be grown so close to central Minneapolis. But it turns out that there are pockets of green all over the city—you just need to know where to look.

5 One final point: I couldn't believe how pricey my weekly grocery shopping trip was this week. Normally, it's about $40, but this week, it was more than $55 for more or less the same amount of food. Any ideas why?

TwinCitiesMom   October 10

Hi—regarding your last point, I've found the same thing recently. I read somewhere that the average "shopping cart" has already increased by 20% this year. The prices have gone up so much because of the awful weather we've been having, and they may go up even more. How are we supposed to feed our families?

 57   11 replies

Ecovore   October 10

I'm not sure we should be supporting restaurants like Moda. They are very bad for the environment. What about all the extra carbon emissions from the transportation that's required to bring over those ingredients from Turkey? That kind of transportation wastes fuel and creates pollution.

 81   5 replies

Anonymous   October 11

I know what you're saying, Ecovore, but you can't just blame places like Moda. If we grow exotic vegetables in Minnesota, then we have to use heated greenhouses, and that probably uses even more energy.

 102   25 replies

---

[1]prides itself on (phr v) is proud of

[2]locally sourced (adj) originating from a nearby location; not requiring lengthy transportation

WHILE READING

3 ANNOTATING **Read the blog on pages 18–19. Check your predictions in Exercise 2. Highlight information in the blog that supports the correct answers.**

4 READING FOR DETAILS **Answer the questions with information from the blog.**

1 Why does the blog's author like Moda?

_____

2 What is the main selling point of Chez Fitz?

_____

3 What question does the blogger ask at the end of the post?

_____

4 What is TwinCitiesMom angry about?

_____

5 **Read the blog again. Write *T* (true), *F* (false), or *DNS* (does not say) next to the statements. Correct the false statements.**

_____ 1 It is impossible to grow food in urban areas.

_____ 2 The author has noticed an increase of almost 40% in the cost of food.

_____ 3 Restaurants like Chez Fitz will become more common in the future.

_____ 4 Chez Fitz tries to minimize food transportation that wastes fuel and creates pollution.

_____ 5 Food prices are going up in Turkey.

_____ 6 To eat at Moda regularly, you would have to be relatively wealthy.

READING BETWEEN THE LINES

6 WORKING OUT MEANING **The blog author uses informal language. Match informal words and phrases to formal words. Use the context to help you.**

1 kick off   a expensive

2 pricey   b import

3 bring over   c begin

7 MAKING INFERENCES **Work with a partner. Discuss the questions.**

1 Do you think the blog author likes *perfectionists*?

2 Why do you think the chef gave a discount to the blog's readers?

3 Why do you think the blogger's shopping trip was more expensive?

◌̇ CRITICAL THINKING

8 **Work with a partner. Discuss the questions.**

APPLY	ANALYZE	EVALUATE
Do you read blogs or reviews online? Why or why not?	What kind of information should be in a restaurant review? Why?	Should you believe restaurant reviews you read online? Why or why not?

COLLABORATION

9 **A** Work in a small group. Choose a restaurant that you know. Complete the T-chart with things you like and the things you dislike about the restaurant.

Name of restaurant:	
Likes	Dislikes

B Write a review of the restaurant for a food blog. Use Reading 1 as a model.

C Share your reviews with the class. As a class, decide which restaurant you would most like to visit.

PREPARING TO READ

 1 UNDERSTANDING KEY VOCABULARY **Read the definitions. Complete the sentences with the correct form of the words in bold.**

> **consumption** (n) the using of goods and services in an economy
>
> **convenience** (n) something that is suitable to your purposes and causes no difficulty for your schedule or plans
>
> **ensure** (v) to make certain that something is done or happens
>
> **experiment** (v) to test or to try a new way of doing something
>
> **increase** (v) to become larger or greater
>
> **influence** (n) the power to have an effect on people or things, or someone or something that is able to do this
>
> **relatively** (adv) quite good, bad, etc. in comparison with other similar things or with what you would expect
>
> **specialty** (n) a product that is unusually good in a particular place

1 Many shoppers have switched to ordering groceries online because of its _____. Now they don't leave their homes to buy food.

2 Others, however, prefer to see the food before they buy it to _____ that the food is fresh.

3 People sometimes reduce their _____ of certain foods when those foods become more expensive.

4 If bad weather affects the supply of some fruits or vegetables, it can cause their prices to _____ .

5 People who live in big cities tend to be _____ familiar with international food compared to people who live in rural areas.

6   Larger cities often have more _____ food stores, which sell foreign
    and less-familiar items.

7   Recently, the popularity of cooking programs on television has had a big
    _____ on the ingredients that people use. People want to cook with
    foods they see on TV.

8   Some travelers like to eat familiar food, but others prefer to _____
    with unfamiliar dishes.

SCANNING TOPIC SENTENCES

Good paragraphs in formal, academic writing usually start with *topic sentences.*
These tell you the subject of the paragraph. By reading the first sentence of each
paragraph in a text, you can often get a good idea of the overall content and also
which paragraph to look at if you need some specific information.

2   SCANNING TO FIND MAIN IDEAS   **You are going to read an essay about changing eating habits
    in Italy. Read the topic sentences. Work with a partner and discuss what you think the
    rest of each paragraph will be about.**

    1   In Italy, changing trends have affected the preparation of food.

    2   Italians' food tastes have changed because of globalization.

    3   A third major change in Italy's food culture has been the rise of large restaurant chains.

3   **After you read the essay on pages 24–25, check your answers from Exercise 2.**

CHANGING EATING HABITS in ITALY

WHAT IS THE COST OF GLOBALIZATION?

1 Globalization is causing a lot of change in international culture, from the TV shows we watch to the clothes we wear. One major area that has been affected by globalization is food culture. In a recent survey taken in Japan, Brazil, and Canada, 72% of people said that globalization had improved their eating habits. It seems clear that globalization has significantly affected food **consumption** in most parts of the world, but one country whose food has a long history of being "globalized" is Italy. If you walk down any main street in any major world city, you will find at least one Italian restaurant. Furthermore, Italy has seen changes in its own eating habits due to **influence** from other countries. This influence, which is a result of the broader trend of globalization, has had both advantages and disadvantages.

2 In Italy, changing trends have affected the preparation of food. Italian families have always taken a lot of pride in preparing food. Until recently, pasta—a basic Italian food—would have been made by people in their local area. Families would also have made the sauces to eat with the pasta at home. People no longer spend so much time preparing their meals. Indeed, frozen or take-out Italian meals have become very popular in Italy. Furthermore, dried pasta is now mass-produced[1] and is sold **relatively** cheaply in supermarkets. Ready-made pasta sauces are also increasingly popular—sales have doubled in the last five years, according to one manufacturer. This has added to the convenience of making meals, but has diminished[2] a cultural tradition.

3 Italians' food tastes have changed because of globalization. People are traveling more, being exposed to other cultures more, and reading about and seeing foreign ingredients and recipes on the Internet and social media. Immigrants to Italy bring their food traditions with them. It used to be that people's opportunities to **experiment** with foreign food were very limited, since only pizza and pasta were available in the local town square. Now they can eat at restaurants with foreign cuisine[3] and buy foreign food in shops. Indian, Chinese, and Japanese food have all become especially popular. While this trend is more common in urban areas such as Rome, Milan, and Venice, many smaller towns are also experiencing similar changes. Many Italians would say that this has been a positive change, but others worry that they are losing their sense of nationality as foreign food becomes more common.

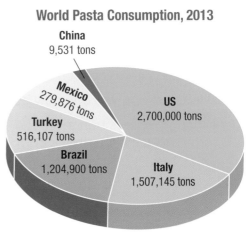

World Pasta Consumption, 2013

China
9,531 tons

Mexico
279,876 tons

Turkey
516,107 tons

Brazil
1,204,900 tons

US
2,700,000 tons

Italy
1,507,145 tons

Source: *World Pasta Organisation*

4 A third major change in Italy's food culture has been the rise of large restaurant chains. These chains are often foreign, and their numbers have **increased** enormously in recent years. Many people like the **convenience** of fast food. Some Italians, however, feel that this has resulted in the destruction of local and national **specialties**. In 1986, a famous fast-food chain opened a restaurant in a historic Rome neighborhood. Many unhappy people responded by joining the "Slow Food" movement. This movement encourages people to eat healthy, locally sourced food.

5 In summary, globalization has had a significant effect on the way that Italians eat. Its influence can be seen as both positive and negative. Convenience foods have replaced many of the traditional home-cooked meals, and the availability of foreign foods and international chains has greatly increased. Italians no longer have to rely on food that is produced locally. While some people welcome this extra choice, others fear the damage it may cause to Italian traditions, culture, and local businesses. On the other hand, the great popularity of Italian food worldwide will **ensure** this great cuisine never disappears.

[1] mass-produced (adj) made in large amounts, using machinery in a factory

[2] diminished (v) made smaller; decreased

[3] cuisine (n) style of cooking

4 READING FOR MAIN IDEAS **Read the essay. Do the topics in the table refer to the past, the present, or both? Check (✓) the correct column.**

		past	present	both
1	mass production of pasta		✓	
2	making pasta sauce at home			
3	popularity of frozen food			
4	lack of foreign food in Italy			
5	the rise of large restaurant chains			
6	worldwide popularity of Italian food			

5 PARAPHRASING **Complete the sentences with your own words.**

1   Italian restaurants can be found _____.

2   In the past, it was not common for Italians to _____.

3   In Italian shops, you can now buy _____.

4   Although recent changes mean Italians have more time and more choice, some dislike the fact that local food is _____.

SKILLS

TAKING NOTES ON SUPPORTING EXAMPLES

Academic writers provide supporting examples for their statements or opinions to show that they are true. Look for supporting examples when you take notes. Tables and diagrams can help you organize your notes.

6 TAKING NOTES **Read the statements. Find and highlight examples in Reading 2 that support the statements in the table. Then complete the student notes.**

statement	supporting examples
Italians pride themselves on preparing food.	– homemade pasta & sauce
In the past, the opportunity to experiment with foreign food was limited.	– people traveled less – only pizza & pasta available locally
People spend less time preparing food now than in the past.	
Italians worry that they are losing their sense of nationality.	
Globalization has become a significant influence in Italy.	

READING BETWEEN THE LINES

7 IDENTIFYING PURPOSE AND AUDIENCE **Work with a partner. Discuss the questions and choose the best answer.**

1 What types of readers do you think this essay is meant to appeal to?

   a people who have a general interest in food

   b people who are experts in Italian food

2 What do you think is the author's main intention in writing this essay?

   a to say that globalization has had a largely positive impact on Italian food

   b to say that globalization has fundamentally changed Italian food

CRITICAL THINKING

8 SYNTHESIZING **Work with a partner. Use ideas from Reading 1 and Reading 2 to discuss the questions.**

ANALYZE

Should governments limit the growth of multinational restaurant chains to allow local, traditional restaurants to compete for customers?

EVALUATE

When you eat at a foreign food restaurant, which of these three qualities is most important to you: that it is *inexpensive*, *locally owned*, or *authentic*? Why?

COLLABORATION

9 **A** Work with a partner. Imagine you want to open a restaurant. Choose the type of restaurant. Then create a market research survey with 5-10 questions to find out information to make your restaurant successful. Think about:

   • location   • food

   • hours   • design

   • cost   • advertising

B Survey five people, and report the results to the class.

C As a class, discuss the results, and decide which restaurant to open.

ACADEMIC ALTERNATIVES TO PHRASAL VERBS

LANGUAGE

Academic writers usually use language that is more formal than spoken language or language in informal pieces.

Phrasal verbs, which usually consist of a main verb followed by a particle (e.g., *up, on*), are often used informally but are less common in academic texts. Instead, a phrasal verb is often replaced by a single, more formal academic word.

1 **Match the phrasal verbs to the academic verbs.**

1	go on	a	increase
2	go up	b	continue
3	turn down	c	study
4	look into	d	confuse
5	use up	e	remove
6	mix up	f	refuse
7	leave out	g	exclude
8	take away	h	exhaust

2 **Replace the phrasal verbs in bold with the correct form of the academic verbs from Exercise 1.**

1 The amount of migrant labor is expected to **go up**. _____

2 If multinational companies **go on** expanding, smaller local suppliers may die out. _____

3 Academics have been **looking into** the implications of globalization for many years. _____

4 Immigration can lead to people becoming **mixed up** about their sense of nationality. _____

5 Although many people benefit from globalization, others can also be **left out**. _____

6 Immigrants without suitable qualifications may have their visa requests **turned down**.

7 When a country's natural resources are **used up**, they may need to rely on other countries to supply them. _____

8 Some supporters of global economic freedom believe that all trade barriers should be **taken away**. _____

GLOBALIZATION VOCABULARY

3 **Complete the text about globalization with words from the box.**

consumption diets farms monopoly multinational
obesity outlets poverty supermarkets

There are both advantages and disadvantages of globalization in terms of food. On the negative side, (1)_____ companies have been criticized for opening too many fast-food (2)_____ in developing countries. This is causing (3)_____ in children, who are becoming addicted to a fatty, westernized diet. Many of these companies are able to effectively set whatever price they like for the food because they have a (4)_____ . Their goods are cheaper than healthier local products and appeal to people living in (5)_____ .

On the other hand, globalization means that people now have the possibility of more variety in their (6)_____ . The development of large-scale (7)_____ and fisheries means some products are more affordable and can allow people to eat protein-rich foods on a regular basis for the first time. Large amounts of this food can often be bought cheaply by big (8)_____ and then sold to customers at a reasonable price. Because of these changes, (9)_____ of products such as meat has increased throughout the world.

WATCH AND LISTEN

taste buds (n)   the cells on your tongue that allow you to taste different foods

boundary (n)   a line that divides two areas or forms an edge around an area

spectrum (n)   a range of objects, ideas, or opinions

squid (n)   a sea animal with a long body and te arms that can shoot out black ink

wacky (adj)   strange or unusual in a surprising c silly way

craving (n)   a strong feeling that you want or ne a particular thing

PREPARING TO WATCH

1   ACTIVATING YOUR KNOWLEDGE   **Work with a partner. Discuss the questions.**

1   What do people mean when they say that the world is getting smaller?

2   What products do you have that were made in another country?

3   What are the pros and cons of importing and exporting products?

2   PREDICTING CONTENT USING VISUALS   **Look at the pictures from the video. Discuss the questions with your partner.**

1   Which of these companies do you know?

2   Which products from these companies are popular in your country?

WHILE WATCHING

3   UNDERSTANDING MAIN IDEAS   **Watch the video. Write *T* (true), *F* (false), or *DNS* (does not say) next to the statements. Correct the false statements.**

_____   1   American food companies are increasing their sales in China every year.

_____   2   Chinese consumers only like salty products from U.S. brands.

_____   3   Many of these flavors are popular with American consumers.

_____   4   The Chinese consumer market is expected to grow in the future.

_____   5   American grocery stores are building branches in China.

4 UNDERSTANDING DETAILS **Watch again. Complete the student's notes with words from the box.**

| American   competitive   popular   sweet   unique |

– examples of (1)_____ brands in China: Cheetos, Minute Maid, Frito-Lay
– (2)_____ Frito-Lay flavor in U.S.: sour cream & onion
– Frito-Lay flavors in China: Szechuan spicy, (3)_____ & sour tomato, cucumber, lychee, mango
– Chinese market = very (4)_____
– U.S. chains sell (5)_____ products in China

5 MAKING INFERENCES **Read the sentences from the video. Choose the best meaning from the box for each phrase in italics.**

| a   expand what is possible
  b   become part of
  c   all kinds of products |

1 Every major U.S. food label, it seems, is trying to *bite into* China's $186 billon food industry. _____

2 It's Frito-Lay potato chips that really *push the boundaries* [of flavor]. _____

3 *Every corner* of the grocery store is trying to tempt China's curious consumers. _____

CRITICAL THINKING

6 **Work in a small group. Discuss the questions.**

UNDERSTAND

Which products in the video seem unusual to you? Would you be interested in trying them?

UNDERSTAND

Which products do not appeal to you? Why not?

ANALYZE

What are three ways that a company might change a product to appeal to a new market? Explain your answers.

COLLABORATION

7 **A** Work with a partner. Make a list of four things besides food that are strongly affected by globalization. Brainstorm at least three effects or examples of effects for each one.

B Share your list and notes with another group. Are there more advantages or disadvantages to globalization?

C As a group of four, share your conclusion and reasons with the class.

EDUCATION

LEARNING OBJECTIVES

Key Reading Skill	Making inferences; using a Venn diagram
Additional Reading Skills	Understanding key vocabulary; using your knowledge; reading for main ideas; reading for details; taking notes; synthesizing
Language Development	Education vocabulary; academic words

ACTIVATE YOUR KNOWLEDGE

Work with a partner. Discuss the questions.

1   What exams do high school students in your country have to take?

2   Is there anything in your country's education system you would like to change? Why or why not?

3   What kind of technology do students in your country use? How can technology improve education?

4   Learning to do a specific skilled job, such as machine repair or farm work, is called *vocational training*. What are some advantages or disadvantages of vocational training over academic college study?

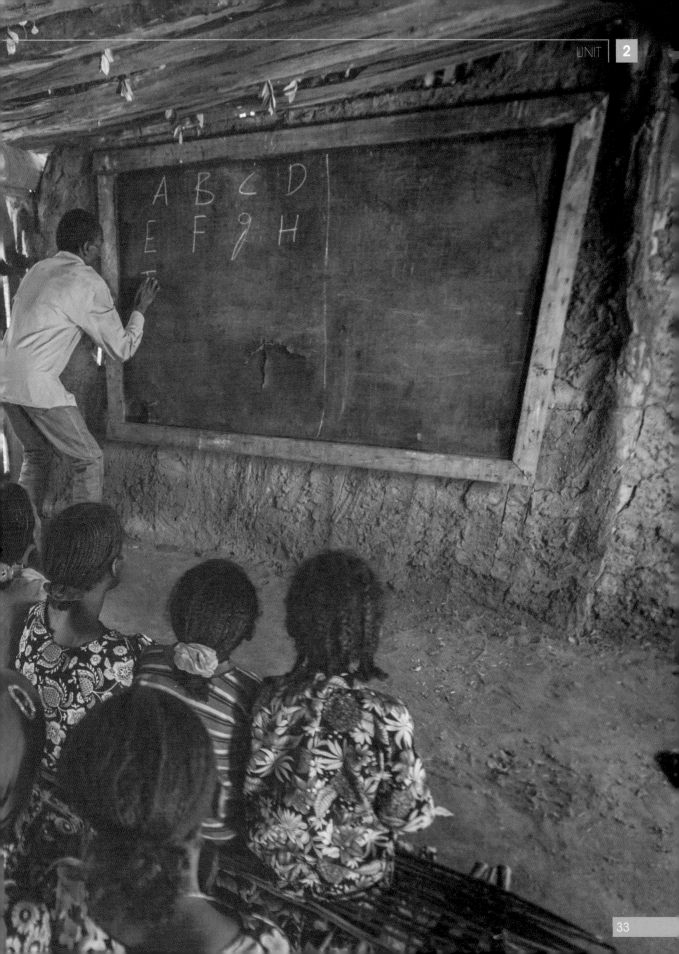

PREPARING TO READ

1 UNDERSTANDING KEY VOCABULARY **Read the sentences. Write the words in bold next to the definitions.**

1 When you want to support your opinion in an essay, it is good to provide **concrete** examples to support it rather than simply giving your general point of view.

2 In October, the university will **launch** a new program to use more solar energy.

3 Chemistry and physics are related, but they are taught as separate scientific **disciplines**.

4 If you want to **pursue** a career in politics, political science is a good subject to study.

5 Some schools are more **oriented** toward science learning than others.

6 There is a large **gender gap** in science and engineering education. However, governments and universities are trying to attract more female students to these subjects.

7 Some people feel that students from lower-income families are **underrepresented** at the best universities.

8 As distance education **evolves**, more and more people may get academic degrees online.

a _____ (v) to try to do or achieve

b _____ (adj) based on actual things and particular examples

c _____ (v) to begin or introduce a new plan

d _____ (adj) directed toward or focused on

e _____ (adj) not given enough presence; in unreasonably lower numbers than others

f _____ (v) to change or develop gradually

g _____ (n) a particular area of study

h _____ (n) the difference in opportunities, attitudes, pay, etc. between men and women

2 Read the sentences. The words and phrases in bold are the *opposites* of the words in bold from Exercise 1. Write the words from Exercise 1 next to their opposites.

1   I started medical school, but it was not right for me, so I decided to **quit** the program. _____pursue_____

2   Cooking is a **non-academic topic** that you cannot study at a major college or university. _____

3   There is an **equal male-to-female ratio** at my college. _____

4   The university will **end** its marketing campaign in June. _____

5   Mechanical engineering classes are usually **not directed toward** literature majors.
    _____

6   Every physics professor at the college attended the meeting, so that department was a bit **overrepresented**. _____

7   You cannot tell what objects the artist is trying to paint in her work. Her paintings are very **abstract**. _____

8   If you do not read the latest research in your field, your career may suffer and **stop developing**. _____

3 USING YOUR KNOWLEDGE   Circle the answers that are true for you. Then compare with a partner.

1   Do you know anyone who has majored in, or plans to major in, business?

    a   yes   b   no   c   not sure

2   Do you know anyone who has majored in, or plans to major in, engineering?

    a   yes   b   no   c   not sure

3   Which one do you think is a more difficult subject to study?

    a   engineering   b   business   c   they are equally difficult

4   Which one do you think is better preparation for finding a job after college?

    a   engineering   b   business   c   they are equal

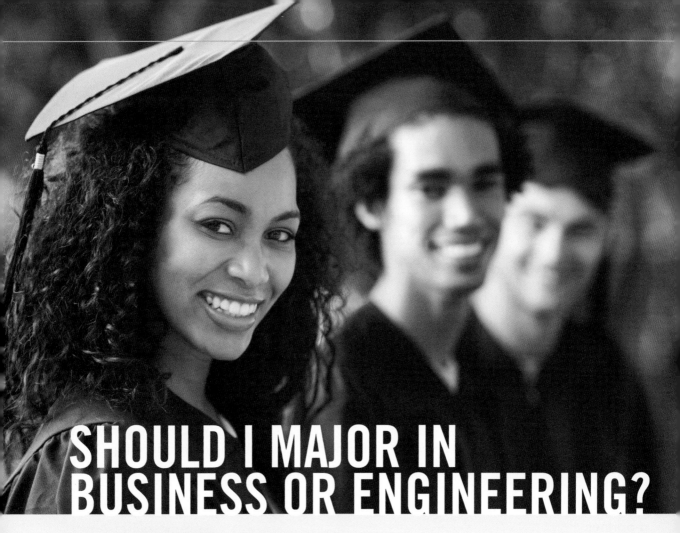

SHOULD I MAJOR IN BUSINESS OR ENGINEERING?

IT ALL DEPENDS...

Choosing a Major

1 Perhaps the most important decision a college student has to make is what subject to major in. Most colleges offer a wide variety of interesting subjects from which to choose, so for some students the choice can be difficult. Some students want to follow their academic interests and major in something that is not directly linked to a future career, such as history or philosophy. Others are looking for a degree in a practical subject that provides **concrete** skills for the working world. For these students, subjects like business and engineering are attractive options. Despite this common ground, however, there are significant differences between these two majors in terms of their popularity and the gender ratio of students.

Majors to Launch a Career

2 Both business and engineering are viewed as majors that will help students **launch** their careers after graduation, but these **disciplines** also provide a good foundation for continued study in graduate school. Many students who **pursue** an MBA[1] feel that the best way to get into a good program is to study business and management in college. Students who want to get a graduate degree in engineering will have a hard time with the subject if they have not already taken engineering courses in college, which is different from degrees more **oriented** toward the humanities[2]. Finally, both areas require the use of mathematics. Business majors will need to be able to work with budgets and financial and accounting ideas, and engineers rely on mathematical calculations for their work.

Gender Differences among Majors

3 On the other hand, these two majors differ quite a bit—both in terms of their popularity and the presence of a **gender gap**. By all measures, business is the most popular major for U.S. college students overall. Engineering subjects, in contrast, are much less popular. Of the engineering degrees, mechanical engineering is the most popular, ranked 26th. Electrical engineering is 31st, and civil engineering is 42nd. Other engineering majors are below the top 50. In terms of gender balance, many college majors are commonly more popular with one gender than the other, but business majors are split about evenly between male and female students. When asked why they have chosen business, many women say that they want to study something that makes them employable but that also focuses on communication skills. In the case of engineering, which has less of a focus on communication skills, only 14% of students are women, according to the American Society of Engineering Education. Engineering is the E in the acronym STEM, which stands for science, technology, engineering, and mathematics. For male students, engineering is the most popular STEM major, while for female students it is biology. There are different theories about why women are so **underrepresented** in engineering, and in STEM in general. Some people think that it is simply because fewer women are interested in these fields, while others think that young girls may be discouraged by parents, teachers, and society in general from pursuing STEM occupations. Even though women make up 47% of all U.S. employees, only 14% of engineers are women. In certain fields, such as mechanical engineering, the percentage is even less than 10%.

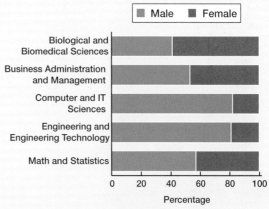

Conclusion

4 To conclude, business and engineering are both practical, career-oriented majors that are attractive to U.S. college students, but which differ in significant ways. Business, the most popular major, has a 50–50 split between male and female students. Engineering, in contrast, is less popular with women—86% of its majors are male students. As perceptions of men and women continue to change in the United States, and as the job market **evolves**, it will be interesting to see if these trends continue or change.

Gender Distribution of U.S. Graduates in Popular STEM Majors, 2014—2015

■ Male ■ Female

- Biological and Biomedical Sciences
- Business Administration and Management
- Computer and IT Sciences
- Engineering and Engineering Technology
- Math and Statistics

0   20   40   60   80   100
Percentage

Source: National Center for Education Statistics

¹MBA (Masters of Business Administration) (n) an advanced degree in business

²humanities (n) literature, language, history, philosophy, and other subjects that are not a science

4 READING FOR MAIN IDEAS **Read the article on pages 36–37. Are the statements below about business, engineering, or both? Check (✓) the correct column.**

		business	engineering	both
1	will help students launch their careers			
2	has a gender gap			
3	is the most popular U.S. college major			
4	is a STEM subject			
5	requires the use of mathematics			
6	provides a good foundation for graduate school			
7	involves working with electronics and mechanics			

 5 READING FOR DETAILS **Work with a partner. Answer the questions about the article.**

1 Which majors are mentioned as examples of ones which are not directly linked to careers?

_____

_____

2 What suggestion is given for people who plan to attend graduate school for engineering?

_____

_____

3 What is the most popular engineering major in the U.S.?

_____

4 What percentage of U.S. engineers are women?

_____

READING BETWEEN THE LINES

 SKILLS

MAKING INFERENCES

Sometimes writers suggest the meaning of something without saying it directly. Being able to read this inferred meaning (as well as the literal meaning of the words) is a useful skill. Practice using reasoning, logic, and your knowledge of the world to work out the real meaning behind the words you read.

6 MAKING INFERENCES **Work with a partner. Discuss the questions.**

1 Why would a student prefer to major in a career-oriented subject?

2 What are disadvantages of majoring in business or engineering?

⚙ CRITICAL THINKING

7 Work with a partner. Discuss the questions.

APPLY	ANALYZE	CREATE
Are you interested in STEM subjects? Why?	Is there a gender balance in STEM education in your country? Explain your answer.	What are three policies that colleges could use to decrease the gender gap in STEM and business programs?

🖧 COLLABORATION

8 A Work in a group of four. *How important is it to choose a major that is linked to your future career?* Assign each student to find one of the following:

- three advantages of choosing a major linked to a career
- three advantages of choosing a major not linked to a career
- three disadvantages of choosing a major linked to a career
- three disadvantages of choosing a major not linked to a career

B Discuss your ideas and reasons with your group. Add two advantages or disadvantages to each list.

C As a group, choose one position and present it to the class. Answer questions at the end of your presentation.

PREPARING TO READ

1 UNDERSTANDING KEY VOCABULARY **Read the collocations and their meanings. Then complete the sentences with your own words.**

> **core principles** (n phr)   key values
>
> **credible alternative** (n phr)   reliable substitute
>
> **distance learning** (n phr)   general education from online instruction
>
> **modern phenomenon** (n phr)   recent trend
>
> **online degree** (n phr)   an academic qualification obtained from online instruction
>
> **significant difference** (n phr)   important distinction
>
> **technological advances** (n phr)   developments in technology
>
> **virtual classroom** (n phr)   online course

1   One interesting **modern phenomenon** in my country is _____ _____ .

2   A subject that might not work well for **distance learning** is _____ _____ .

3   One advantage of a real classroom over a **virtual classroom** is _____ _____ .

4   One advantage of an **online degree** over a degree that requires attending classes is _____ _____ .

5   It's possible that a **credible alternative** to gasoline might be _____

   _____ .

6   Because of **technological advances**, it is now much easier to _____

   _____ .

7   One of the **core principles** of many colleges is _____

   _____ .

8   One **significant difference** between high school and college is _____

   _____ .

2   USING YOUR KNOWLEDGE   **Write A (agree) or D (disagree) next to the statements to show your opinion. Discuss your answers with a partner.**

_____   1   Distance learning is a new idea.

_____   2   Distance learning requires good technological access.

_____   3   Face-to-face learning is better than distance learning.

3   **After you read the article on pages 42–43, check your answers to Exercise 2.**

Distance Learning vs. Face-to-Face Learning

1 Although many people think it is a **modern phenomenon**, **distance learning** has been around for at least 200 years in one form or another. Historical examples of long-distance learning include students being sent a series of weekly lessons by mail. The **technological advances** of the past 20 or so years, however, have meant that this form of education is now a **credible alternative** to face-to-face learning. Indeed, 1996 saw the establishment of the world's first "virtual university" in the United States, showing how far distance learning has come in a relatively short space of time. While it is now possible to obtain a large variety of **online degrees**, which is the best type of education to pursue? A closer examination of this topic reveals that distance and traditional educational instruction have **significant differences** but also some similarities.

"
distance learning has been around for at least 200 years

2 When comparing the two systems, the most obvious difference lies in the way that instruction is delivered. Distance learning is heavily dependent on technology, particularly the Internet. In a face-to-face course, students may only require a computer for the purpose of writing an essay. In comparison, when learning remotely, technology is the principal means of communication. Face-to-face instruction must take place in real time and in one location. Conversely, distance learning can happen at any time and in any location, since the learning is not restricted by geography. The flexibility this provides means that students may be better able to learn at their own pace, but it may also mean that learners have to be well organized and self-disciplined. In other words, they must be more highly motivated in order to do well in distance-learning courses. Finally, with face-to-face learning, the teacher and student have the opportunity to develop a personal relationship. In a **virtual classroom**, by contrast, the teacher may seldom or never actually meet the student. This may make it hard for teachers to understand their students' specific learning needs.

3 Although the nature of the teacher-student relationship may differ in the two methods, they do share the same **core principles**. Just as a teacher is the "knower" in a classroom, he or she is the one responsible for helping students understand the key sections of an online course. The teacher needs to decide how to best present the material to be learned and in which sequence the topics should be introduced. He or she must also create the assignments for the course and help the students know what resources (textbooks, websites, and so on) will best support their learning. Additionally, a teacher needs to provide student feedback in some way. For example, a language teacher in a classroom may be able to correct a student's grammar or pronunciation in the moment, whereas a distance-learning teacher may need to provide written or recorded feedback to be delivered later. In any case, all the usual elements of the teacher's role are necessary, no matter what kind of instruction is being used.

4 It is difficult to state whether one form of learning is better than another, since they are geared toward different learning situations. They are certainly different experiences. Nevertheless, there are strong similarities between the two systems, which can both produce positive results. A student who has the choice should consider the advantages and disadvantages of each method before deciding to take a course.

More than a quarter of higher education students are enrolled in at least one online course. –EdTech

4 READING FOR MAIN IDEAS **Write the correct paragraph number next to the description.**

1 Similarities between the two methods   Paragraph: _____

2 General summary and conclusions   Paragraph: _____

3 Differences between the methods   Paragraph: _____

4 The history and background of the topic Paragraph: _____

5 READING FOR DETAILS **Are the statements about distance learning, face-to-face learning, or both? Check (✔) the correct column.**

		distance learning	face-to-face learning	both
1	develops a strong student-teacher relationship			
2	relies heavily on technology			
3	flexible with time			
4	can be an effective way of teaching			
5	requires a high level of motivation			
6	not limited by geography			
7	can suit many types of students			

✎ SKILLS

USING A VENN DIAGRAM

A Venn diagram is useful for taking notes on similarities and differences. It consists of two or three overlapping circles. Write down important points for what you are comparing in the outside circles. Then look for similarities and write them in the inside circle.

6 TAKING NOTES **Find and highlight points of comparison between distance and face-to-face learning in the text. Take notes in a Venn diagram like the one below.**

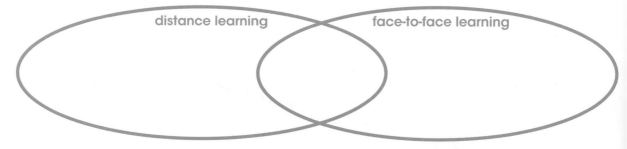

distance learning   face-to-face learning

READING BETWEEN THE LINES

7 MAKING INFERENCES **Work with a partner. Answer the questions.**

1   Why do some people think distance learning is a modern idea?

_____

_____

2   Why can online learning be slightly impersonal?

_____

_____

3   How would teacher feedback differ between the two methods in a
language course?

_____

_____

4   Does the author of the article generally approve or disapprove of distance learning?

_____

_____

ᕯ CRITICAL THINKING

8 SYNTHESIZING **Work with a partner. Use ideas from Reading 1 and Reading 2 to discuss
the questions.**

APPLY	ANALYZE	EVALUATE
Have you ever tried to learn something online? What were the advantages and disadvantages of doing this?	Are there any problems with face-to-face teaching?	How do you think teaching should change in the future?

COLLABORATION

9 **A**   Which do you think would work better with distance learning: a STEM course or a
language course? Choose a side, and make a list of reasons to support it.

B   Find two or three students who chose the same side. Discuss and combine your top
five reasons.

C   Divide the class into two sides, the pro-STEM and the pro-language students. Have
an informal debate. Your teacher will moderate and decide the winner.

EDUCATION VOCABULARY

1 **Complete each sentence with a word from the box. Use a dictionary to help you.**

> assignment   degree   journal   teaching   assistant
> plagiarism   semester   seminar   tutor

1 The work required of students in college is a(n) _____ .

2 An academic year can be divided into two periods, each called a(n) _____ .

3 _____ is when students copy from or do not acknowledge their sources when writing an essay.

4 A(n) _____ is a quarterly, peer-reviewed collection of research papers.

5 A(n) _____ is a graduate student who teaches classes at a college or university.

6 A(n) _____ is a short course or meeting where people discuss a particular subject.

7 A(n) _____ works with a student one-on-one on a specific academic skill.

8 When you have completed a program of study at a college or university, you get a(n) _____ .

ACADEMIC WORDS

2 **Match the academic words to the definitions.**

1 alternative   a the foundation or starting of an organization

2 establishment   b part or feature of something

3 virtual   c enthusiasm for doing something

4 significant   d different from something else

5 core   e particular or exact

6 principle   f existing in a technological environment

7 specific   g important or noticeable

8 motivation   h the most important part of something

9 aspect   i a basic idea or rule

3 **Complete the sentences with the correct forms of some of the words from Exercise 2.**

1 Many students prefer to study a job-related subject as a(n) _____ to an academic course.

2 The flexibility offered by distance learning is seen as a(n) _____ benefit by many students.

3 One beneficial _____ of university education is meeting the other students in the course.

4 Tutors work with students to help them understand the key _____ of their courses.

5 Distance learning requires students to have a high level of _____ .

6 Distance learning can make it hard for a teacher to understand a student's _____ learning needs.

7 As well as taking _____ modules, students will be able to take other optional elective classes in various areas.

8 1996 saw the establishment of the world's first _____ university, which operated only on the Internet.

GLOSSARY

mortgage (n)   an agreement that allows you to borrow money from a bank to buy a house

federal (adj)   related to the national government

variable (adj)   able to change or be changed

bankruptcy (n)   the inability to pay your debts

harass (v)   to annoy or trouble someone, often repeatedly

testify (v)   to tell what you know about something in an official situation, like a court of law

repeal (v)   to officially make a law end

fine print (n)   important information that is often printed in small letters in an agreement or official document

PREPARING TO WATCH

1 ACTIVATING YOUR KNOWLEDGE **Work with a partner. Discuss the questions.**

1   How many years does the average student spend in each of the following: kindergarten, elementary school, middle school, high school, college, graduate school?

2   How do most students pay for college?

3   Would you consider getting a loan to pay for college? Why or why not?

2 PREDICTING CONTENT USING VISUALS **Look at the pictures from the video. Check (✓) the ideas that you expect to hear.**

1   ☐   Getting a college degree will help your family.

2   ☐   Students are investing thousands of dollars in their college education.

3   ☐   Students are borrowing more money for college than ever before.

4   ☐   Borrowing money without understanding all the details can cause financial problems.

5   ☐   The costs of higher education in the United States can cause financial stress for many students.

WHILE WATCHING

3 UNDERSTANDING MAIN IDEAS **Watch the video. Answer the questions.**

1 Which of your predictions from Exercise 2 were correct?

2 Which sentence best represents the main idea of the video?

   a Borrowing money for college does not always pay off.

   b Before borrowing money for college tuition, it is essential to understand the details of the loan.

   c It is better to get a mortgage than to get a student loan.

4 SUMMARIZING **Watch again. Complete the summary.**

> Velicia Cooks completed her college degree with $80,000 worth of (1) _____ .
> She represents typical students graduating today. On average, students graduate with
> (2) _____ of debt. However, many students like Velicia are unaware of the
> (3) _____ between federal and private loans. Private loans can cost a student
> (4) _____ times the amount of the original loan. This may lead a graduate to file for
> (5) _____ , but education debt stays with you. Reading the (6) _____ is
> important in understanding the financial responsibilities that go along with taking a loan.

☼ CRITICAL THINKING

5 **Work with a partner. Discuss the questions.**

APPLY	ANALYZE	EVALUATE
Why is paying for college so difficult in the United States? Is it the same in other countries?	Is it the government's responsibility to prevent situations like Velicia's? Why or why not?	What, if anything, should be done to make college tuition more affordable?

COLLABORATION

6 A Work in a small group. Brainstorm a list of the advantages and a list of the disadvantages of getting a college degree. Think about:

• Type of degree   • Time   • Personal goals

• Cost   • Career

B Interview five people with jobs and a college degree about the advantages and disadvantages. Revise your lists if necessary.

C As a group, choose a position and write a two-minute script to support it. Your goal is to convince people either to go to college or to do something else. Video and/or perform your "pitch" to the class.

MEDICINE

Key Reading Skill	Annotating a text
Additional Reading Skills	Understanding key vocabulary; using your knowledge; previewing; reading for details; identifying opinions; skimming; reading for main ideas; scanning to find key words; making inferences; synthesizing
Language Development	Medical vocabulary; academic vocabulary

ACTIVATE YOUR KNOWLEDGE

Work with a partner. Discuss the questions.

1 What is the best treatment for:

   • a cold?   • depression?

   • a headache?   • stress?

2 Do you think medicine from a doctor is the best remedy for the medical problems above?

3 What other types of treatment are there besides conventional medication available from a doctor?

4 Would you use alternative medicine to treat a serious illness? Why or why not?

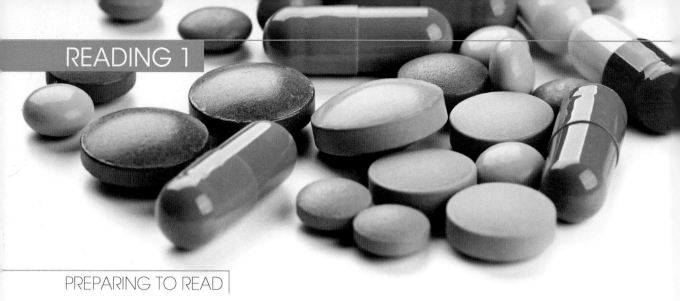

PREPARING TO READ

1 UNDERSTANDING KEY VOCABULARY **Read the sentences and choose the best definition for the words in bold.**

1 After my knee **surgery**, my leg was sore for several weeks.
  a taking medicine for a period of time after you are sick
  b the cutting open of the body to repair a damaged part

2 Two **symptoms** of the common cold are coughing and sneezing.
  a types of illnesses
  b reactions or feelings of illness that are caused by a disease

3 Doctors are usually big **proponents** of regular exercise for their patients.
  a people who support a particular idea or plan of action
  b people who argue against an idea

4 The new treatment is **controversial**. Some people think it has not been tested enough, while others believe in it.
  a causing disagreement or discussion
  b causing agreement

5 The government has **funded** the hospital in my neighborhood.
  a given land for a new building
  b provided money to pay for something

6 It is dangerous to consume illegal **substances** because they have not been approved by the country's medical authorities.
  a foods that are unhealthy
  b materials with particular physical characteristics

7 My grandmother is afraid to use **conventional** treatment for her illness. Instead, she drinks a tea made from a variety of plants.
  a following the usual practices
  b alternative and non-traditional

8 Heart disease is the **chief** cause of death for people in the United States.
  a most important or main
  b most uncommon

2 USING YOUR KNOWLEDGE   **Work with a partner. Look at the chart. Add at least five more illnesses or diseases and ways to prevent them.**

Illness	Prevention
the flu	get a flu shot

3 PREVIEWING   **Look at the title, subheads, and introduction of Reading 1. Decide which statement best describes what the article is about.**

1   The article presents the arguments for and against conventional types of medicine.

2   The article discusses why some alternative medical treatments are free.

3   The article gives two people's opinions on the effectiveness of using homeopathy.

4   The article discusses a range of alternative medical treatments.

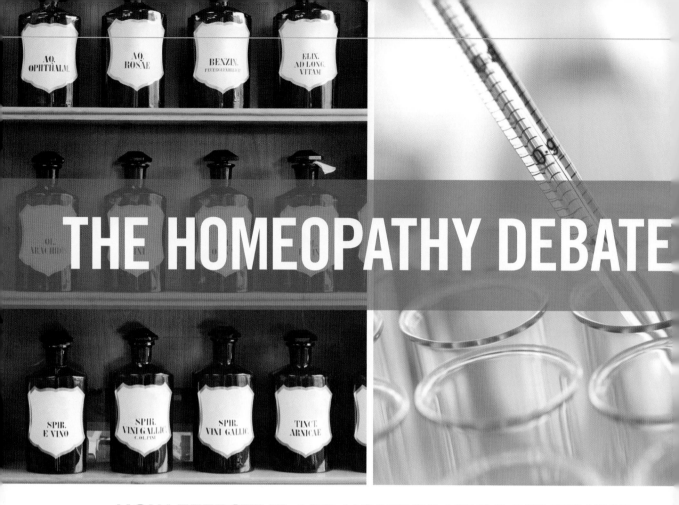

THE HOMEOPATHY DEBATE

HOW EFFECTIVE ARE HOMEOPATHIC REMEDIES?

1 Most national healthcare programs use **conventional** medicine, meaning that illnesses are treated using drugs and **surgery**. However, there is also a range of alternative medical treatments to choose from. One **controversial** treatment is homeopathy. Homeopathic remedies are highly diluted[1] mixtures of natural **substances**, such as plants and minerals, that may cause the **symptoms** of a disease in healthy people. The idea is that they will cure similar symptoms in sick people. Supporters of homeopathy believe that it can be effective. Others argue, however, that homeopathy does not work and agree that they should not be **funded** by government programs such as Medicare and Medicaid in the United States (national health insurance programs for seniors, people with disabilities, and low-income families). Here, one **proponent** and one critic present their cases.

[1] **diluted** (adj) made weaker by mixing with something else, such as water
[2] **placebo effect** (n) an improvement in a patient's condition caused only by his or her belief in the benefit of the treatment

Homeopathy Should Be Covered by Government Healthcare Programs
by Jessica Noguera (Professional Homeopath)

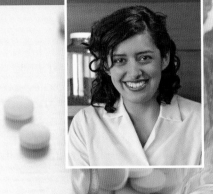

2 In 1810, a German physician named Samuel Hahnemann published an overview of his medical theories and research in a book titled *The Organon of the Healing Art*, which stated that consuming a substance that causes the symptoms of an illness could cure that illness. This was the birth of homeopathy. Ever since then, many people have tried this alternative treatment and found success with it. Often, homeopathic treatment is less expensive than conventional medicine is, since it is made from plants and other natural substances. Also, but perhaps less importantly, over 400 doctors in the United States regularly recommend homeopathic treatments. Since they are cheap and popular, I find it difficult to understand why Medicare and Medicaid do not fund them. Why shouldn't people be allowed to make their own health choices? They have this freedom in other aspects of their lives—for example, which school to send their children to—so why not in terms of their healthcare?

3 As for the critics who argue that homeopathy doesn't work, I could give hundreds of examples of patients who have been cured by my treatment. On top of that, there's plenty of research that shows the benefits it can bring. Homeopathy wouldn't have survived so long if it were complete nonsense. It has much more than just a placebo effect[2]. Too much emphasis is sometimes put on providing "proof" of why something works. Belief is just as powerful.

Homeopathy Should Not Be Covered by Government Healthcare Programs
by Dr. Piers Wehner (Primary Care Physician)

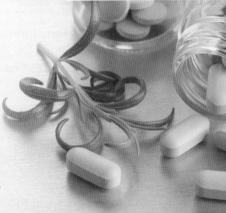

4 We don't really know whether homeopathy helps people feel better because of the remedies themselves or because people believe they will work. Some people just feel better when they get personal care and attention from their homeopathic practitioner. For me and many others in my profession, there is absolutely no proof that says homeopathic treatment works. The government's **chief** scientist confirmed this when he said there was "no real evidence" to support homeopathy. We live in difficult economic times, and every health insurance penny the government spends should be checked to ensure that it is not wasted. In fact, 75% of U.S. doctors are against the use of Medicare and Medicaid for funding of homeopathy.

5 One of the main arguments put forward by supporters of homeopathy is that this therapy doesn't cause any damage. However, people may think they are treating their illness by taking homeopathic remedies when there is actually no scientific evidence that this is true. Even more seriously, patients who rely on homeopathy alone for treating life-threatening illnesses like cancer could be taking a big risk. The cancer might no longer be treatable by proven methods if the patient has waited too long trying homeopathy. This can cost lives.

SKILLS

ANNOTATING A TEXT

Annotating a text while you read can help you remember information a lot better. When you annotate, you mark up the text and add notes in the margin as you read. When you read about different writers' opinions on a single subject, it is a good idea to highlight each writer's opinions in a different color, then underline the support each writer gives for their opinions. You can also react to a writer's opinions by writing notes in the margin, putting a star next to the strongest reasons and support, etc.

4 ANNOTATING **Read the article on the homeopathy debate. Highlight each writer's opinion in a different color and underline the support each writer provides. Write notes in the margin as you read.**

5 READING FOR DETAILS **Read the article again. Write *T* (true), *F* (false), or *DNS* (does not say) next to the statements. Correct the false statements.**

_____ 1 The majority of countries use alternative rather than conventional medicine.

_____ 2 Supporters of homeopathy believe that patients should have choices in their treatment.

_____ 3 More than two-thirds of doctors in the United States are against homeopathic treatment.

_____ 4 Traditional Indian doctors frequently use homeopathy.

_____ 5 Jessica Nogueira thinks that homeopathic remedies only work because of the placebo effect.

_____ 6 Medicare and Medicaid do not fund homeopathic remedies.

_____ 7 Homeopathic health care is not available in the United States.

_____ 8 Weak, highly diluted liquids are a common form of homeopathic treatment.

READING BETWEEN THE LINES

6 IDENTIFYING OPINIONS **Which of the two people in the article would agree with the statements?**

		Jessica Nogueira	Piers Wehner
1	The doctor says it's too late to help her now. If only she'd gone to see him earlier.		
2	Look, if I don't want to risk the side effects of conventional drugs, why should I have to?		
3	When I see proper clinical trials that prove the effectiveness of homeopathy, *then* I'll change my mind.		
4	The mind has incredibly strong healing powers.		
5	If it means we could stop paying all that money for drugs, then I'm for it.		
6	It worked. I don't know why. It doesn't seem possible, but I'm just happy that it worked.		
7	This is serious. You can keep taking the homeopathic treatment as well, if you want, but you've got to see a doctor.		
8	If three-quarters of professionals are against it, I'm against it.		

⚗ CRITICAL THINKING

7 **Work with a partner. Discuss the questions.**

APPLY

Why do you think alternative medicines are popular with some people?

APPLY

Do you think alternative medicine only creates a placebo effect?

ANALYZE

Do you think some medicines that are considered alternative in one society might be considered conventional in another? Give examples.

COLLABORATION

8 A Read the statements. Check the ones you agree with. Put an X beside the ones you disagree with. Make notes on your reasons.

- *Belief is as powerful as medicine.*
- *There is no real proof that homeopathy works.*
- *Homeopathic medicine works.*

B Work with a partner. Compare your ideas. Try to persuade your partner to agree with you.

C Repeat step B with at least three more people.

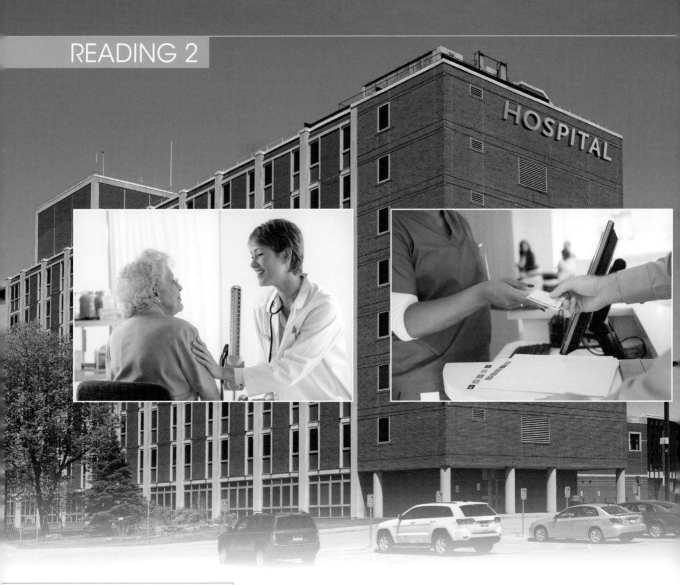

PREPARING TO READ

1 UNDERSTANDING KEY VOCABULARY **Read the definitions. Complete the sentences on page 59 with the correct form of the words in bold.**

burden (n) a duty or responsibility that is hard to bear

consultation (n) a meeting with a doctor who is specially trained to give advice to you or other doctors about an illness

contribution (n) money, support, or other help

labor (n) practical work, especially work that involves physical effort

regardless (adv) despite; not being affected by something

safety net (n) something used to protect a person against possible hardship or difficulty

treatment (n) the use of drugs, exercise, etc. to improve the condition of a sick or injured person, or to cure a disease

1   When elderly people get sick, it sometimes places a financial _____ on
    their adult children, who have to help pay for expensive treatments.

2   After three months of _____, the patient can now walk well.

3   Everybody must pay their share, _____ of how much they earn.

4   It is a good idea to save some money as a(n) _____, just in case you lose
    your job.

5   The doctor examined me when I went to her for a(n) _____ about
    my symptoms.

6   We each gave a(n) _____ of money to send our sick coworker
    some flowers.

7   When you calculate the price of building a new hospital, you have to consider
    materials and also the cost of _____ .

2   USING YOUR KNOWLEDGE   **Work with a partner. Answer the questions.**

1   Do you have to pay for health care in your country?

    _____

    _____

2   What health care provision, if any, does your government pay for?

    _____

    _____

3   Should everybody be able to access free health care?

    _____

    _____

3   SKIMMING   **Skim the blog on pages
60–61. Read the title, introduction,
and topic sentences. Decide which
statement best describes what the
blog is about.**

1   The blog examines different kinds
    of public health care in different
    countries.

2   The blog focuses on private funding
    as it relates to health care.

3   The blog criticizes government
    policies.

4   The blog discusses the role of
    medication in health care.

SHOULD HEALTH CARE BE FREE?

More information

FOLLOWERS
201k

ELSEWHERE

1| Who pays for health care? The answer varies from country to country. In the United States, people often receive their health insurance through their employer. In other places, health care is completely free for all residents. There are also places where you can only see a doctor if you pay. Often, a patient is faced with the choice of medium-quality but cheap care versus high-quality but expensive care. Unfortunately, providing health care to an entire nation of citizens is a complicated matter. While different health care systems have various advantages and disadvantages, no system is ideal.

2| FREE OR PUBLIC HEALTH CARE Within the countries that provide free public health care, there are many models. In some countries, **consultations**, **treatment**, and medicines are free to all citizens. This may be paid for directly by the government, perhaps funded by the country's valuable natural resources that the government owns. Other countries collect money from citizens through taxes based on their income. Workers pay according to how much they earn, and employers also make a **contribution**. Hospitals and other medical services are then provided and run by the government. There may also be some private medical services that people can choose to buy. The advantage of systems such as these is clear: free basic health care for all, **regardless** of income. However, it is a very expensive system and, as life expectancy and costs rise, many countries are facing either an unsustainable financial **burden**, or a drop in the quality of services and facilities provided.

3| PRIVATE HEALTH CARE In countries where citizens use private providers, health care is only available to patients who pay for it, and health care providers are commercial companies. In wealthier countries, most citizens take out health insurance to cover their potential medical costs. However, not everyone can afford this, and some governments have a program that gives financial assistance to those who need urgent medical care but are unable to afford it. In other nations, there is no such **safety net**, and those who cannot pay simply do not get the health care they need, unless they can get help. The disadvantages of this system are obvious: not only are individuals deprived of the medical attention they need, but also the lack of preventative medicine means that infectious diseases can quickly spread. One advantage, however, is that commercial organizations can sometimes provide higher-quality care than struggling government-funded ones.

Countries with free healthcare (2017)

4| A MIXED SYSTEM   In many countries, there is a mix of public and private funding. This system requires all its citizens to take out health insurance. This is deducted from salaries by the employer, who also has to make a contribution for each worker. Citizens are able to choose their health care providers, which may be public or private. However, in some systems, private companies are not permitted to make a profit from providing basic health care. This model provides more flexibility than either the public or private models, and ensures access to health care for all. However, it has been criticized for driving up the cost of **labor**, which can lead to unemployment.

5| CONCLUSION   Most of us will likely agree that no health care system is perfect. Several countries are now considering a combination of the models for their national health systems. The challenge is to find a system that provides a high-quality level of health care to all citizens, but which is also affordable and practical. Whether or not such as system can work remains to be seen.

John K   October 10

It's crazy to have citizens in a free country pay such high prices for health care. The system must change! Only the government can help pay the cost of medical care for its citizens.

 73   11 replies

Becky   October 10

People need to take care of themselves. My tax dollars can go to better things than paying for you if you're sick. I wouldn't want you to pay for me!

 7   5 replies

4 READING FOR MAIN IDEAS   **Read the blog on pages 60–61. Answer the questions.**

1   Which of the three systems described is most similar to the one your country follows? Are there any differences?

2   Which system gives people the best access to health care? The best quality health care?

3   How do people in the United States feel about the health care debate?

5 READING FOR DETAILS   **Read the blog again. Identify which system (public, private, or mixed) in the blog these countries use.**

1   **The United Kingdom** Under this country's National Health Service (NHS), all workers pay National Insurance according to how much they earn. This is collected by the government and is used to pay for hospitals and other medical treatment. Most of this is free, except for prescriptions, eye care, and dental care. Most hospitals are owned and run by the government.

_____

2   **The Democratic Republic of Congo** Here, many people do not have access to a doctor and in some areas there is an insufficient supply of medicine. Doctors are typically paid in cash, and even those who do manage to see a doctor often cannot afford the treatment.

_____

3   **Qatar** This country spends more on health care per person than any other country in the Gulf region. Health care is free (or almost free) for everyone. This is paid for by the government.

_____

4   **The United States** Here, health care is expensive. Over 11% of Americans do not have health coverage. Those who are not enrolled in government programs like Medicare or Medicaid usually have to pay for some kind of health insurance.

_____

5   **Germany** Here, most workers have to pay for government health insurance from their salaries or buy insurance on their own.

_____

6 SCANNING TO FIND KEY WORDS   **Scan the blog quickly to find words to complete the table.**

synonyms of *people*	
synonyms of *money*	
related to *health care*	

READING BETWEEN THE LINES

7 MAKING INFERENCES **Work with a partner. Answer the questions based on information in the blog.**

1 Which health care system might a person with a long-term illness prefer? Why?

_____

_____

2 Which system might a person with a high income prefer? Why?

_____

_____

☀ CRITICAL THINKING

8 SYNTHESIZING **Work with a partner. Use ideas from Reading 1 and Reading 2 to discuss the questions.**

APPLY

Do you know of any health care treatments that people sometimes use in your country that might be considered alternative or unconventional?

ANALYZE

Why do you think different countries have different health care systems?

EVALUATE

In countries where the government pays for everyone's health care, should alternative treatments such as homeopathy be covered? Why or why not?

⚅ COLLABORATION

9 A Work with a partner. What types of medical care should be the responsibility of the individual — for example, physical therapy, massage, acupuncture, surgery, dental, vision, etc.? What should be the responsibility of the government? What should be both the government's and individual's responsibility? Complete the Venn diagram.

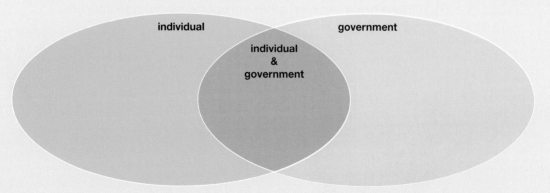

B Share your diagram with another group. Discuss your reasons. Do you agree?

MEDICAL VOCABULARY

1 Read the definitions. Complete the sentences with the correct form of the words in bold.

> **drug dependency** (n)   being unable to function normally without a particular type of medicine
>
> **epidemic** (n)   an illness that affects large numbers of people at the same time
>
> **patent** (n)   the official legal right to make or sell an invention for a particular number of years
>
> **preventable illness** (n)   a disease that can be avoided, often by a person looking after themselves better
>
> **sedentary lifestyle** (n)   a way of life that does not involve much activity or exercise
>
> **underfunding** (n)   lack of money provided for something, often academic or scientific research

1   Following a national emergency such as an earthquake, clean water must be restored quickly to prevent the spread of a(n) _____ .

2   A decrease in spending by the government means hospitals suffer from _____ .

3   _____ can occur when people are prescribed a medicine for a long time.

4   The rise in obesity, particularly among young people, is often the result of a(n) _____ .

5   A lack of exercise and eating the wrong food can lead to the development of a(n) _____ such as diabetes.

6   Pharmaceutical companies have _____ on their new drugs, but once these have expired, other companies can manufacture and market the same drugs.

ACADEMIC VOCABULARY

2 **Write the correct adjective forms of the academic nouns in the table.**

adjective	definition	noun
1	having a negative or harmful effect on something	adversity
2	having the qualities that you connect with trained and skilled people	profession
3	against the law	illegality
4	connected with the body	physicality
5	difficult to understand or find an answer to because of having many different parts	complexity
6	enough or satisfactory for a particular purpose	adequacy
7	traditional and ordinary	convention
8	exact and accurate	precision
9	related to the treatment of illness and injuries	medicine

3 **Circle the correct word to complete each sentence.**

1 Many countries are fighting against the growing use of *complex* / *illegal* drugs.

2 Doctors and nurses are two examples of *precision* / *professional* health care practitioners.

3 People have the right to expect *illegal* / *adequate* service from doctors and nurses.

4 *Conventional* / *Professional* medicine involves the use of drugs, unlike alternative forms of medicine.

5 Several surgeons may be needed in *complex* / *adverse* medical operations.

6 Health systems should focus on the treatment of mental conditions, as well as *physical* / *conventional* health care.

7 Hospitals can suffer *illegal* / *adverse* conditions such as underfunding or overcrowding.

8 It takes many years of *medical* / *professional* study to become a doctor.

9 When giving drugs to patients, it is crucially important that the quantity provided is *adequate* / *precise*.

WATCH AND LISTEN

PREPARING TO WATCH

1 ACTIVATING YOUR KNOWLEDGE   **Work with a partner. Discuss the questions.**

1   What kinds of allergies can people have?

2   Do you know anyone with an allergy? What happens when they have an allergic reaction?

3   How would you feel if you had to get a shot or injection every week?

4   Is alternative medicine a good choice for people with allergies? Why or why not?

2 PREDICTING CONTENT USING VISUALS   **Look at the pictures from the video. Make predictions with your partner.**

1   What do you think is special about the toothpaste?

2   What do you think the scientist is putting in the toothpaste?

3   What medical condition could the man have?

4   How might the toothpaste help him?

WHILE WATCHING

3 UNDERSTANDING MAIN IDEAS **Watch the video. Number the statements in the order they are mentioned.**

a   Derek is treating his allergies while he is brushing his teeth.   _____

b   Dr. Reisacher created Allerdent.   _____

c   The toothpaste, Allerdent, contains extracts of allergens.   _____

d   Allerdent has helped Derek.   _____

e   Derek is part of a study testing the new toothpaste.   _____

4 UNDERSTANDING DETAILS **Watch again. Answer the questions.**

a   What is Derek allergic to? _____

b   How many patients are testing the new toothpaste? _____

c   What two traditional treatments can Allerdent replace? _____

d   How many allergies can Allerdent treat at one time? _____

5 MAKING INFERENCES **Work with a partner. Put a check (✓) next to the statements that you can infer from the video. Give reasons for your answers.**

1   ☐   Customizing medicine is beneficial for patients.

2   ☐   More people are likely to prefer toothpaste to weekly shots.

3   ☐   Using extracts from plants is better for one's health.

4   ☐   Allergens are increasing.

☀ CRITICAL THINKING

6 **Work with a partner. Discuss the questions.**

APPLY

Do you have any allergies? How would your life be different if they could be cured?

EVALUATE

Are there any disadvantages to using toothpaste to deliver a person's medication? Describe them.

COLLABORATION

7 A   Work in a small group. Think of three common products that could be used to deliver medication. Write down advantages and disadvantages for each one.

B   Share your list with another group. Choose one product and create a short marketing presentation for it.

C   As a group, present your product to the class. As a class, vote on the top three ideas.

THE ENVIRONMENT

LEARNING OBJECTIVES

Key Reading Skill	Identifying cohesive devices
Additional Reading Skills	Understanding key vocabulary; predicting content using visuals; reading for details; making inferences; using your knowledge; reading for main ideas; taking notes; synthesizing
Language Development	Academic noun phrases; natural disaster vocabulary

ACTIVATE YOUR KNOWLEDGE

Work with a partner. Discuss the questions.

1 Why do floods (large amounts of water covering a normally dry area) and droughts (long periods with little or no rain) occur? What impact can they have on a country?

2 Look at the photo. How often do floods like this happen in your city or country?

3 What other natural disasters do you know about? What impact do they have on people and places?

PREPARING TO READ

1 UNDERSTANDING KEY VOCABULARY **Read the two paragraphs and write each bold word next to the correct definition.**

> **A**   Scientists have not yet **identified** which kind of storm is approaching the Caribbean. The last storm was a hurricane that had a **devastating** effect on the buildings near the beach, as many of them were destroyed. To prepare for this storm, there are several important **measures** that people in that area should take. For example, it is **crucial** to have plenty of water, some flashlights, and batteries.

1 _____ (n) a method for dealing with a situation

2 _____ (v) to recognize something and say what that thing is

3 _____ (adj) extremely important or necessary

4 _____ (adj) causing a lot of damage or destruction

> **B**   Our **community** is located by the ocean and contains about 75 families. We are all working toward a **reduction** in the damage done by storms here. Part of that includes sharing the **maintenance** costs of planting sea grass and building sand fences. In the past, some families were **criticized** for not contributing their fair share of these maintenance costs.

5 _____ (n) the people living in one particular area

6 _____ (n) the work needed to keep something in good condition

7 _____ (n) the act of making something smaller in size or amount

8 _____ (v) to express disapproval of someone or something

2 PREDICTING CONTENT USING VISUALS **Before you read the interview on pages 72–73, look at the photos on page 71 of different types of natural disasters and ways to prevent damage from these events. Label the photos with the words from the box.**

dam   levee   flood barrier   hurricane   sandbagging   tsunami

1

4

2

5

3

6

IN A RECENT 10-YEAR PERIOD, NATURAL DISASTERS CAUSED OVER $1.5 TRILLION (US) IN DAMAGE, AND MORE THAN ONE MILLION HUMAN DEATHS.

CONTROLLING CERTAIN DISASTER

Water Management Monthly interviews Dan Smith

1 The world has always had to face water-based natural disasters such as tsunamis and hurricanes. In an illuminating[1] interview, *Water Management Monthly* talks to Dan Smith, who works in disaster mitigation for a government agency.

Dan, could you tell us what *disaster mitigation* means?

Disaster mitigation means attempting to minimize the impact of natural disasters both before and after they happen. My department and I work in <u>two specific areas</u> to try and do this: risk **reduction** and risk analysis. Both are **crucial** in disaster mitigation.

What do you mean by *risk reduction*?

Risk reduction means many things. <u>It</u> is not just referring to big engineering projects like dams. Often, small **community** projects can be the most effective means of risk reduction. The main way floods can be prevented is by the construction and **maintenance** of earth-wall defenses, or levees. <u>These</u> block the progress of rising water. However, even the best levees can't protect against the **devastating** power of a tsunami. In <u>this case</u>, early-warning systems are lifesavers. They can let people know as early as possible if there is likely to be flooding.

What types of risk analysis do you do?

Thames Barrier

First, risk analysis concerns flood mapping, where we **identify** the parts of the country that are at most risk from flooding. Second, there is mitigation planning, which helps local communities plan for when disaster strikes. Third, <u>we</u> make sure that the country's dams all work properly and are safe. Although many people **criticize** dams because of their environmental impact, they also have many benefits such as hydroelectricity, irrigation, water storage, water sports, and, of course, flood control. In terms of a cost-benefit analysis, we are definitely ahead.

Do you think countries are better prepared now for natural disasters than they were in the past?

Definitely. We are constantly developing new flood-prevention solutions. Some examples of <u>these kinds of</u> **measures** include the construction of sea walls and bulkheads[2], which protect the coasts, and the redesign of power stations and subway tunnels in the New York City (NYC) area after the devastating damage caused by Hurricane Sandy in 2012. In the U.K., another good example is the Thames Barrier, a huge engineering project designed to prevent London from flooding.

Aren't programs like <u>that</u> very expensive? What lower-cost alternatives are there?

NYC subway tunnel

Flood prevention does not have to be expensive. Sandbags, for example, can be a highly effective way of stopping flood water.

Is there any more that can be done, or are we as prepared as we can be?

There's always more that could be done. But remember that the government can only be responsible for flood prevention up to a certain point. People have to become aware of the dangers of flooding themselves. This is crucial. Expensive early-warning systems are a waste of money if people pay no attention to <u>them</u>.

[1] **illuminating** (adj) giving you new information about a subject
[2] **bulkhead** (n) an underwater wall

3 READING FOR DETAILS **Read the interview again. Write *T* (true), *F* (false), or *DNS* (does not say) next to the statements. Correct the false statements.**

_____ 1 Dan Smith works for an international organization.

_____ 2 Risk reduction and risk analysis are both important parts of disaster mitigation.

_____ 3 Large-scale projects are always effective for risk reduction.

_____ 4 Planning for natural disasters has improved in recent years.

_____ 5 The New York City subway tunnel redesign cost $20 million.

_____ 6 Low-technology solutions can protect against flooding, too.

🛠 SKILLS

IDENTIFYING COHESIVE DEVICES

Good academic writing flows easily and is not too repetitive. The writer needs to show links between ideas without repeating the same words. Using pronouns and synonyms in the place of nouns and noun phrases can help. To read well in English, you need to be able to identify what these pronouns and synonyms refer to.

Droughts often occur in <u>central Kenya</u>. **This area** is so dry that it cannot support crops.

In order to avoid repetition, the writer refers back to central Kenya with a pronoun in a new noun phrase: "*this* area."

<u>Droughts</u> can also cause people to suffer if the **lack of water** means that people don't have enough to drink.

Here, the writer refers back to the idea of droughts with a synonym phrase: "lack of water."

---

4 INDENTIFYING COHESIVE DEVICES **Find these words and phrases underlined in the interview. Write the nouns or noun phrases that they refer to.**

1 two specific areas _____

2 It _____

3 These _____

4 this case _____

5 we _____

6 these kinds of measures _____

7 that _____

8 them _____

READING BETWEEN THE LINES

5 MAKING INFERENCES **Work with a partner. Which of the opinions do you think Dan Smith would agree with? Explain your reasons.**

1   It's the government's responsibility to protect us from natural disasters.

2   Surely it's more important to spend time and money on ways to stop water from causing floods, rather than finding out which areas are likely to flood. We already know that.

3   Dams are more trouble than they're worth.

4   Building sea walls is a waste of money—sandbags are just as good.

5   People in flood-risk areas need to be educated about the risks and about how they can help themselves.

☼ CRITICAL THINKING

6 **Work with a partner. Discuss the questions.**

APPLY	ANALYZE	EVALUATE
Does your country ever have problems with flooding? If so, how do people protect themselves?	How would life in your country be different if you had higher or lower rainfall?	Which countries have particularly serious problems with flooding? Explain your reasons.

COLLABORATION

7 A   Work in a small group. Choose a city that is threatened by flooding. Do some research. Create a fact sheet or poster to help educate people who live in the city. Include:

- the greatest areas, people, and infrastructure at risk
- ways to pay for prevention

- ways to reduce the risks
- photos or illustrations

B   Present your fact sheet or poster to the class. Include time for questions and answers at the end of your presentation.

PREPARING TO READ

1 UNDERSTANDING KEY VOCABULARY **You are going to read a report on drought in rural Africa. Read the definitions. Complete the sentences with the correct form of the words in bold.**

> **casualty** (n)   a person hurt or killed in a serious accident or event
>
> **disrupt** (v)   to prevent something from continuing as expected
>
> **infrastructure** (n)   the basic systems and services, such as transportation and power, that a country uses to work effectively
>
> **issue** (n)   a subject or problem that people are thinking about or discussing
>
> **monitor** (v)   to watch and check something carefully over a period of time
>
> **policy** (n)   a set of ideas or a plan for action that a business, government, political party, or group of people follow
>
> **rely on** (phr v)   to depend on or trust someone or something
>
> **strategy** (n)   a long-range plan for achieving a goal

1   A hurricane _____ our vacation to the Caribbean, and we had to return home sooner than expected.

2   The local government was relieved that were no _____ in the earthquake. Everyone was safe.

3   There are several effective _____ for preventing coastal damage from high waves and flood water, such as planting sea grass, using sandbags, and constructing sea walls and bulkheads.

4   Environmental pollution is a(n) _____ that more people are paying attention to. There is more recycling and less use of plastic.

5   Companies are now asked to _____ their greenhouse gas emissions to make sure they are not too high.

6   Some environmentalists don't think we should just _____ the government to regulate pollution. They believe we need citizens to be involved as well.

7   Developing countries often lack a strong enough _____ to be able to provide water and electricity to all residents.

8   The Environmental Protection Agency's _____ is to make sure that the government considers the environmental effects of its plans.

2 PREDICTING CONTENT USING VISUALS **Drought is a major problem in many parts of the world. Look at the map. Identify at least five more countries in each column of the T-chart. Be prepared to explain your answers.**

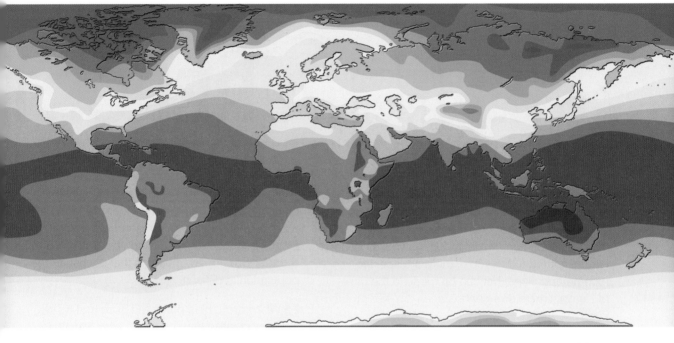

-58 -40 -31 -22 -13 -4   5 14 32   41 50 59 68 77 86 95°F

-50 -40 -35 -30 -25 -20 -15 -10   0   5 10 15 20 25 30 35°C

high risk	low risk
Somalia	Canada

3 USING YOUR KNOWLEDGE **Work with a partner. Discuss the questions.**

1 What are the effects of drought?

2 How can people suffering from drought be helped in the short term?

3 What are some long-term solutions to a shortage of water?

4 Why do developing countries struggle with droughts?

COMBATING DROUGHT in RURAL AFRICA | A REPORT

1 In order to mitigate the problems that drought can bring, there are several short- and long-term **strategies** that can be adopted. A range of **policies** designed to combat these problems exists at local, national, and international levels. As well as general **issues** related to this topic, there are specific recommendations that can be made in the case of Kenya, where drought has been a major problem in recent years.

2 Droughts frequently put millions of people at risk of food insecurity[1] in central Kenya. The area is so dry that it cannot support agricultural crops. There are few permanent rivers, and the seasonal waterways caused by flood waters in the rainy months **disrupt** transportation across the region. The population of this area mainly live off their cattle. Droughts can quickly kill off their animals, which eliminates their main source of income. Finally, because the area is so vast, **infrastructure** is under-developed, meaning that access to the population is difficult.

3 When drought is predicted in central Kenya, it is important to employ short-term preventive measures and be prepared to respond to it as quickly as possible in order to minimize **casualties**. One such measure is recycling water. Recycled water, from the washing of clothes for example, can be given to animals and used to irrigate[2] land. A program of this kind can be achieved in two to three months. To do this on a regional level in central Kenya would only cost about $100,000 per year, which is relatively cost-effective. This water cannot be drunk by people, however. Once drought strikes, the most important response is to transport bottles of drinking water into the drought area. This can be done quickly (within one week), but it is quite expensive. Kenya has 47 million people, and to import bottled water for even a quarter of the population could cost as much as $10 million per year. In addition, since drought also often kills animals and crops, it is also vital to bring food to prevent people from starving.

A Maasai woman collects water for her village.

[1] **food insecurity** (n) the state of being without reliable access to a sufficient quantity of affordable, nutritious food

[2] **irrigate** (v) to supply land with water so that crops and plants will grow

ON KENYA

The Horn of Africa

DJIBOUTI
Addis Ababa
SOMALIA
ETHIOPIA
KENYA Mogadishu
Nairobi
Crisis
Emergency

A goat farmer at Koroli Springs

A sand dam saves water for farming.

4 Drought tends to reoccur in the same central areas of Kenya, so long-term solutions are also necessary. The authorities need to **monitor** droughts and gather relevant data. As they are already being paid for their government jobs, this should not add any extra costs to the national budget. The data can then be used for appropriate planning at the local and national levels. This part costs more, as it involves developing irrigation systems for farming communities, or building canals and dams to benefit villages and cities. This could cost as much as $8 million and take as long as two years. On a micro-scale, the construction of wells can help provide more water at a cost of about $500,000. Once the funding is in place, this can be done immediately. On a wider scale, desalination plants, which remove salt from sea water, also make drinking water available, but at a much higher cost of about seven to ten million dollars. These plants can take years to construct before they are running efficiently— perhaps as long as five years. Additionally, harvesting rainwater lets communities collect and store any rain that does fall. This is less costly, but it depends on the rainfall in the area. Sometimes

Kenyans have to wait months for a rainfall. The majority of these strategies are undoubtedly expensive and may only be affordable for richer countries, which have the technology and expertise to predict and plan for drought more effectively.

5 Poorer countries, on the other hand, are generally unable to afford long-term solutions, and may have to **rely on** international support and charity in the short term. Lack of education and under-developed infrastructure may also hamper some of these projects.

6 Overall, we can see that there are several recommendations that can be made for Kenya's drought problems. First, the provision of training in recycling and harvesting water throughout the country at a local level. Second, the implementation of a well construction program to maximize the amount of water available nationally. Third, a movement to lobby the international community to provide funding for a desalination plant on the coast to ensure that Kenya can always meet its water needs.

4 READING FOR MAIN IDEAS **Read the report on pages 78–79. Write the corresponding paragraph number next to the purpose mentioned in the report.**

a   sets out a number of suggestions   _____

b   considers economic factors in decision-making   _____

c   introduces the main purpose of the text   _____

d   discusses a range of long-term strategies   _____

e   discusses a range of short-term strategies   _____

f   briefs the reader on the effects of drought in Kenya   _____

5 TAKING NOTES **Read the report again. Find and highlight these six strategies for dealing with drought. Write the strategies in the appropriate places in the diagram.**

1   constructing dams

2   rainwater harvesting

3   building wells

4   bringing in drinking water

5   water recycling

6   constructing desalination plants

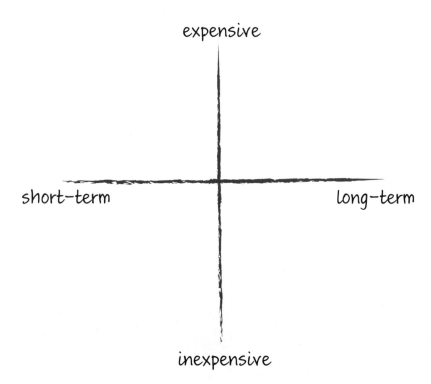

READING BETWEEN THE LINES

6 MAKING INFERENCES **Choose the best answers.**

1 What aspect of this issue does the writer feel is important to understand?

   a the moral challenges of dealing with drought

   b the financial aspects of dealing with drought

2 Why are the people of central Kenya most at risk of drought?

   a their way of life means they need to use a lot of water

   b the area experiences low annual rainfall

3 Which of these points do you think the report's author agrees with most?

   a Partnership between organizations is important in preventing drought.

   b Every country should follow the recommendations in this report.

⌾ CRITICAL THINKING

7 SYNTHESIZING **Work with a partner. Use ideas from Reading 1 and Reading 2 to discuss the questions.**

APPLY	APPLY	EVALUATE
Has your country ever experienced drought? If so, when?	Which strategies mentioned in the text does your country use?	Do you think that future droughts across the world will be more or less severe? Why or why not?

⬡ COLLABORATION

8 A Work in a small group. Do you agree or disagree with the following statement?

Droughts and floods are worse today due to climate change caused by human activity.

Make a list of at least five reasons for and five reasons against the statement.

B Share your ideas with another group. Is there agreement between your groups?

C As a class, discuss what can be done to decrease the number and strength of future floods and droughts. Write a letter or email to the president with your solutions.

LANGUAGE

Two nouns may sometimes be combined in academic writing in order to create a more complex noun phrase that gives greater detail about the subject.

risk + analysis = risk analysis

The meaning of the more complex noun phrase will contain elements of the base nouns.

risk = danger, threat

analysis = the process of looking at something in detail

risk analysis = the process of looking at dangers or threats in detail

When creating noun phrases, it may be necessary to make a noun out of adjectives, verbs, or adverbs (i.e., to *nominalize* them).

manufacture the product = product manufacturing

 1 **Complete each sentence (b) with an academic noun phrase formed from words in each sentence (a).**

1 a We need to mitigate these kinds of disasters.

   b We need ____disaster mitigation____ .

2 a An important component of managing natural disasters is reducing risk.

   b _____ is an important component of managing natural disasters.

3 a It is important for a country to have a system for managing water to protect against flooding.

   b It is important for a country to have a(n) _____ to protect against flooding.

4 a The report made by the government was very influential.

   b The _____ was very influential.

5 a The need for protection against floods is particularly relevant in towns located near rivers.

   b The need for _____ is particularly relevant in towns located near rivers.

6 a Projects based in the community can be effective in minimizing risk.

   b _____ can be effective in minimizing risk.

NATURAL DISASTER VOCABULARY

2 **Look at the adjective-noun collocations. Circle the collocation in each group that has a different meaning.**

1 *natural / terrible / major* disaster

2 *severe / devastating / controlled* flood

3 *ambitious / large-scale / long-term* project

4 *prolonged / seasonal / extreme* drought

3 **Complete the sentences with collocations from Exercise 2. In some cases, more than one answer may be possible.**

1 Due to their complexity, desalination plants are _____ that may take many years to construct.

2 One of the worst _____ in human history was the 1556 earthquake in Shaanxi Province, China.

3 _____ are sometimes used to improve the quality of rivers.

4 _____ such as dams, flood defenses, and early warning systems require huge amounts of investment.

5 In 1931, there was a(n) _____ in China, where more than a million people lost their lives to the water.

6 Due to a very hot climate, sub-Saharan Africa suffers from _____ more than many other places in the world.

7 In an increasing number of places, the lack of winter rain makes the chances of _____ in the summer more likely.

8 Where proper planning has been in place, the chance of a flood or drought turning into a _____ are reduced.

WATCH AND LISTEN

polar ice cap (n)   a thick layer of ice near the North or South Pole that permanently covers an area of land

distribution (n)   the way something is divided and shared in a group or area

transform (v)   to change something completely, often to improve it

reservoir (n)   a natural or artificial lake for storing and supplying water for an area

PREPARING TO WATCH

1 ACTIVATING YOUR KNOWLEDGE   **Check (✓) the statements that you agree with. Compare your answers with a partner.**

1   ☐   There is an unlimited amount of clean drinking water on our planet.

2   ☐   We are losing precious natural resources.

3   ☐   Scientists are developing new ways to clean water.

4   ☐   Desert areas are the only areas in need of more water.

5   ☐   As the population grows, problems with access to clean water increase.

6   ☐   Clean water is used in the production of many goods.

2 PREDICTING CONTENT USING VISUALS   **Look at the pictures from the video. Discuss the questions with your partner.**

1   How much of Earth's surface is water?

2   What parts of the world do you think are experiencing a water shortage?

3   What factors lead to water shortages?

WHILE WATCHING

3 UNDERSTANDING MAIN IDEAS   **Watch the video. Write *T* (true), *F* (false), or *DNS* (does not say) next to the statements. Correct the false statements.**

_____   1   Only 2.5% of Earth's water is available for human use.

_____   2   Transforming deserts, producing energy from rivers, and building cities requires over half of our available fresh water.

_____ 3 Access to clean drinking water is a critical problem for more than a billion people.

_____ 4 Water shortages are simply the result of people living in desert areas.

_____ 5 The Aral Sea now covers 25,000 square miles.

4 SUMMARIZING **Watch again. Complete the summary.**

Water covers about (1)_____ of Earth's surface. However, only a small fraction of this water is suitable for human use. While there is no more water on the planet than there was in the distant past, the (2)_____ of water has changed. This is partly due to an increase in (3)_____ ; as the number of people on the planet grows, so does the water crisis. Several factors contribute to the shortage: poor (4)_____ , politics, poverty, and simply living in a dry part of the world. Cities like Mexico City are especially at risk. Shops that sell water are becoming increasingly (5)_____ . Changes in Earth's water distribution can be seen from (6)_____ . Places like the Aral Sea and Lake Chad in the Sahara Desert have visibly changed due to (7)_____ and overuse.

CRITICAL THINKING

5 **Work with a partner. Discuss the questions.**

UNDERSTAND	ANALYZE	EVALUATE
Why is only a small fraction of Earth's water available for human use?	Is it important for governments to regulate water distribution and use in agriculture and manufacturing?	Clean water has been called the next great resource battle. Do you agree? Why or why not?

COLLABORATION

6 **A** Work in a small group. Make a survey of ten questions about water use and conservation in your class. Include the following questions:

- How often do you purchase bottles of water?
- Are bottles of water environmental problems? If so, how?

B Survey at least five people outside your class. Report the results to your group.

C In your group, make conclusions about water use and conservation based on your survey results. Report your findings to the class.

ARCHITECTURE

LEARNING OBJECTIVES

Key Reading Skill	Skimming a text
Additional Reading Skills	Using your knowledge; understanding key vocabulary; reading for details; annotating; making inferences; summarizing; understanding paraphrase; synthesizing
Language Development	Academic word families; architecture and planning vocabulary

ACTIVATE YOUR KNOWLEDGE

Work with a partner. Discuss the questions.

1 Do people in your country generally live in houses or apartments?

2 What is the most important room in your home? Why?

3 What would you change about your home, school, or workplace to improve it?

4 Are there any famous old buildings in your country? Are they protected? Do you think this is important? Why or why not?

PREPARING TO READ

1 USING YOUR KNOWLEDGE **Work with a partner. Answer the questions.**

1 Which parts of buildings use the most energy?

2 Do you think it is important for new buildings to be environmentally friendly? Why or why not?

3 How can architects design buildings to need less energy in their construction or use?

4 How can we reduce the amount of energy we use in our homes?

2 UNDERSTANDING KEY VOCABULARY **Read the definitions. Complete the sentences with the correct form of the words in bold.**

> **compromise** (n)   an agreement between two sides who have different opinions, in which each side gives up something it had wanted
>
> **conservation** (n)   the protection of plants, animals, and natural areas from the damaging effects of human activity
>
> **durable** (adj)   able to last a long time without being damaged
>
> **efficiency** (n)   the condition or fact of producing the results you want without waste
>
> **relevant** (adj)   related to a subject or to something happening or being discussed
>
> **secondhand** (adj)   not new; having been used in the past by someone else
>
> **sector** (n)   a part of society that can be separated from other parts because of its own special character

1 Buildings that are tough and last a long time are usually made from _____ materials.

2 The city planning committee may have to make a(n) _____ in order to both save money and use high-quality building materials.

3 It is important for developers to consider the _____ of their plan so that they avoid wasting time, money, or labor.

4 Developers cannot build in certain locations, such as rainforests, due to environmental _____.

5 If previously used wood is still in good condition, a builder may choose to use it for construction even though it is _____.

6 Most architects work in the private _____, which means they work for companies and not for the government.

7 The architect who designed the building does not think people's opinion of its appearance is _____ to its purpose.

⚙ SKILLS

SKIMMING A TEXT

Skimming is reading a text quickly in order to get a general idea of its main points. It is particularly useful when you have a great deal of information to read in a short space of time, or when it is not necessary to understand a text in detail. Readers often skim a text to find out if it will be useful or not before reading it more thoroughly. This is particularly important in academic reading where you may only have time to read the most useful texts.

Do ...

✓ look at the title, any subheadings, and illustrations—they will often give clues about the content.

✓ read the introductory paragraph, which should tell you what the text will be about.

✓ read the concluding paragraph.

✓ read the first sentence of each paragraph, which may present its topic.

Don't ...

× stop to look up unknown words.

× say the individual words that you read in your head. Try to just focus on the meaning.

× read examples.

---

3 SKIMMING **Look at the photos with the article on pages 90–91. Read only the title, the introductory paragraph, and the concluding paragraph. Complete the statement below.**

This article will be useful for a student who needs to find out about ...

a   houses in New Mexico.

b   the causes of climate change.

c   the conservation of ancient buildings.

d   arguments for ecologically responsible construction.

4 **How did you find the answer for Exercise 3? What was most helpful—the photos, the title, the introductory paragraph, or the concluding paragraph?**

5 **Skim the article and write the corresponding paragraph numbers next to the ideas below.**

a   a type of eco-building   _____

b   a specific example of an eco-home   _____

c   a current trend in construction   _____

d   the need to produce eco-buildings   _____

e   the pros and cons of producing eco-buildings _____

We Need More
Green Buildings

1 In recent years, there has been a general trend for new buildings to be more environmentally friendly, or more "green." Such a building is sometimes called an *eco-building*. These buildings use energy and water efficiently, which reduces waste and pollution. However, installing features like solar panels and water-recycling systems involves higher construction costs than in a traditional building. Despite these extra costs, green buildings are good for the planet and their benefits are clear.

Earthship house

2 Around the city of Taos, New Mexico, there are many homes, called *Earthship houses*, constructed from recycled bottles, tires, aluminum cans, and other trash. Often the cans, bottles, and tires are filled with soil and then the outsides are covered with natural mud. These homes are designed to use solar power—the energy from the sun—rather than electricity produced from fossil fuels[1]. These recycled-construction designs are just as **relevant** for other types of buildings. In both Uruguay and Sierra Leone, for example, there are recycled-construction schools for local children. The green aspects of this kind of building are relatively inexpensive, and over the life of the building, they should provide a large return on the initial investment[2]. They also function as valuable teaching aids when educating students about the environment.

3 Another example of an eco-building is a private residence in Wales known as the "Hobbit House." Its frame is made of wood and the walls are made of straw, which provides excellent insulation. The roof consists of mud planted with grass, which keeps heat in and has a low impact on the environment. Solar panels provide electricity for lighting and electrical equipment. Water is supplied directly from a nearby river and is also collected from the roof for use in the garden, avoiding the need to waste clean water. Low-impact houses like this one are green because they use **secondhand** materials and do not rely on fossil fuels, but instead use renewable energy sources such as solar or wind power.

Hobbit House

4 Critics of these kinds of eco-buildings say that while they may be good for the environment, there are practical problems with their affordability. They are often too costly to become a large-volume method of construction. There are further concerns over their long-term **efficiency**. Not much energy can be realistically generated by solar panels in places that do not have large amounts of sunlight, and not every location has access to a natural water source. However, overall, green buildings are worth it. Yes, in order to finance environmentally friendly construction and produce an affordable building, **compromises** have to be made. These may be that the building will have to be smaller or made of less **durable** materials and with technology that uses more energy. Perhaps these compromises are easier to make for schools, where ideas about **conservation** are useful for education, or for businesses where ecologically aware features are a useful marketing tool, rather than for private homes.

The construction sector accounts for 30–40% of global energy use.

5 The argument for constructing green buildings is clear. The United Nations Environment Programme estimates that the construction **sector** accounts for 30–40% of global energy use. In some areas, such as the Gulf States, the figure is closer to 50–60%. We need to reduce this energy use for the good of the planet. However, it remains to be seen whether we are able to accept the financial and practical compromises of producing and living in environmentally friendly buildings.

[1] fossil fuels (n) fuels such as gas, coal, and oil produced in the earth from the remains of plants and animals

[2] return on investment (n phr) the benefit to an investor that results from an investment of money

6 READING FOR DETAILS **Read the article on pages 90–91. Write *RC* (recycled-construction building), *HH* (Hobbit House), or *N* (neither type of building) for the architectural features below.**

1 a grass roof _____

2 a local water source _____

3 recycled cans and bottles _____

4 gas heating _____

5 a wooden construction _____

6 straw walls _____

7 recycled tires _____

8 natural insulation _____

7 ANNOTATING **Read the article again. Write *T* (true), *F* (false), or *DNS* (does not say) next to the statements. For all the true and false statements, highlight the sentences in the article that support your answers. Then correct the false statements.**

_____ 1 Generally, eco-buildings are becoming more popular.

_____ 2 Eco-buildings cost double the price of a traditional building.

_____ 3 Environmentally friendly practices are relevant, no matter what size of building you are constructing.

_____ 4 Some old construction methods can be useful in environmentally friendly construction.

_____ 5 Fossil fuels are examples of renewable types of energy.

_____ 6 Some schools are eco-friendly buildings.

_____ 7 The United Nations Environment Programme produces data about global energy use.

READING BETWEEN THE LINES

8 MAKING INFERENCES **Work with a partner. Discuss the questions.**

1 "In recent years there has been a general trend for new buildings to be more environmentally friendly, or more 'green.'" Why do you think this is?

2 The environmental aspects of the recycled-construction school "also function as valuable teaching aids when educating students about the environment." What do you think students learn from the school's environmental aspects?

3 "Not much energy can be realistically generated by solar panels in places that do not have large amounts of sunlight." Why not?

4 How can environmentally friendly aspects of a business be "a useful marketing tool"?

⚡ CRITICAL THINKING

9 **Work with a partner. Discuss the questions.**

APPLY

Would you live in an eco-home if you had to pay more for its environmentally friendly features? Why or why not?

EVALUATE

Do you think there should be restrictions on how much energy individuals or institutions are allowed to use? Why or why not?

🤝 COLLABORATION

10 A Work with a partner. Do you agree or disagree with this statement from the article?

We need to reduce this energy use for the good of the planet.

Brainstorm at least three arguments for and three arguments against reducing energy use. Think of several examples for each argument. After 10-15 minutes, each partner chooses a side.

B Divide the class into two groups, the pros and the cons. Each group prepares an introductory statement, their five best arguments, and a closing statement.

C Have a class debate. Your teacher will moderate and decide the winner.

Storm King Art Center, Mountainville, NY

PREPARING TO READ

1 UNDERSTANDING KEY VOCABULARY **Read the sentences and choose the best definition for the words in bold.**

1 The **function** of an architectural drawing is to show what the building design looks like before it is built.

   a complexity or detail

   b a purpose, or the way something works

2 Buildings that have no windows and are box-like with no unique features or decoration can seem very **depressing**.

   a making you feel unhappy and without hope

   b making you feel physically weak and less active

3 When you see a magnificent work of art, such as a painting or a beautiful building, the creativity behind it can be **inspiring**.

   a causing eagerness to learn or do something

   b informative or educational

4 I felt that the people in that city must be pretty **civilized** when I saw the beautiful parks and buildings that they have.

   a having a well-developed way of life and social systems

   b relating to legal issues

5   It **reflects** badly **on** citizens who do not take care of their public parks and buildings.

   a   reacts to

   b   causes people to think of someone or something in a specified way

6   That architect has a wonderful **reputation** in her field; she is widely admired by many other architects.

   a   the general opinion that people have about someone

   b   a collection of works

7   He **demonstrated** the new construction technique for the public at the building design convention.

   a   criticized or disapproved of something

   b   showed how to do something; explained

2   USING YOUR KNOWLEDGE   **Work with a partner. Discuss the questions. Take notes on your partner's answers.**

1   What are the most beautiful buildings in your country?

   _____

2   Are these buildings older buildings or modern constructions?

   _____

3   Do people in your country generally prefer modern or older houses?

   _____

4   What do people in your country think about modern architecture?

   _____

5   Which is more important for a building: its beauty or its function?

   _____

3   SKIMMING   **Skim the essay on pages 96–97. Does the writer think it is more important to design a building that is beautiful or one that is functional?**

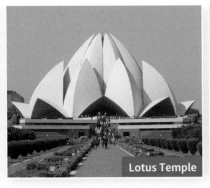
Lotus Temple

Louvre Pyramid

Tokyo Airport

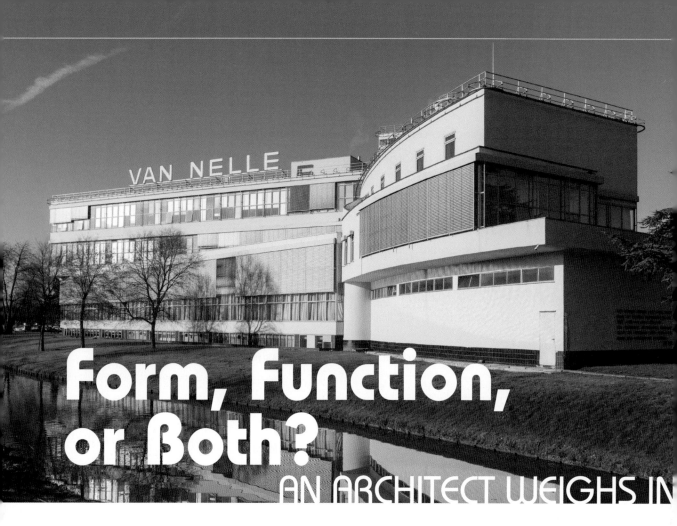

Form, Function, or Both?

AN ARCHITECT WEIGHS IN

1 INTRODUCTION   At the start of the twentieth century, Louis Sullivan, one of the creators of modern architecture, said that "form follows **function**." The term "functionalism" is used to describe the idea behind architecture that primarily focuses on the purpose of a building. However, many people disagree with this and feel that beauty is a more important factor in architectural design. In the modern world, it seems that most architects try to combine both ideas, aiming to create buildings that are both functional and **inspiring** in their beauty. This is often difficult to achieve, however. Since we create buildings to serve the needs in our lives, the importance of function should always be prioritized over form.

Guggenheim Museum, New York, NY

2 HOW IMPORTANT IS BEAUTY?   Many people believe that architects have a wider responsibility to society than just designing functional buildings. Beautiful, well-constructed buildings are a symbol of a **civilized** society and they **reflect** well **on** a business or the **reputation** of the owner. Ugly public buildings, however, can project a negative image of the organization. People say that living or working in an ugly place creates a **depressing** and uninspiring environment. In contrast, an attractive building can make people feel happier and increase their motivation to work.

3 IS FUNCTION IMPORTANT?

While this may be true, the reason for creating a building in the first place—its use—is clearly very important. When building an airport terminal, for example, you need to think of the needs of passengers as well as planes. Passengers want to get to their plane as quickly as they can, and planes need to be parked in a way that maximizes their ease of use. As such, many airport terminals have a circular shape with satellite areas. Residential homes need to have enough space for a family, art galleries need wall space to show pictures, and factories need to produce goods as efficiently as possible. Each type of building has a different function, and, therefore, it has a different form.

Farnsworth House, Plano, IL

4 FORM VS. FUNCTION

In theory, there seems to be no reason why architecture cannot be both functional and beautiful. Yet in practice, this can cause problems. The Modern International style of the 1920s and 1930s, an example of which is the Guggenheim Museum in New York, was supposed to combine beauty with function. Many consider the museum's white spiral ramp beautiful, but there have been complaints that it is impractical, as it is difficult to stand back to view the art. Also, the ramp is so narrow that it can become overcrowded. The Farnsworth House by Ludwig Mies van der Rohe is another icon of beautiful design that **demonstrates** the idea that "less is more." However, critics have attacked it for a lack of privacy because of the huge glass windows. It also has a leaky flat roof and has been repeatedly flooded. It seems that even these two celebrated designs have problems with functionality.

rth House, inside looking out

5 THE FINAL WORD

If architects focus only on function, buildings may be cold, ugly, and uninteresting. There is no doubt that a building with a beautiful form is something we can all appreciate. However, functional needs must be addressed before visual ones. This issue of practicality is the most important feature of the buildings we live in, work in, and visit. Therefore, function must outweigh form when an architect plans a building.

4 SUMMARIZING **Read the essay on pages 96–97. Then complete the summary.**

While some architecture values (1)_____ over form, there is an opposing view that the (2)_____ of a building is more important than its functionality. In practice, most (3)_____ strive for a combination of both ideas.

Architects feel that they are expected to design attractive buildings. The appearance of a building can (4)_____ either positively or negatively on its owner. Also, it can have an impact on the users' (5)_____, which affects motivation.

Still, the first consideration in the design of a (6)_____ should be its purpose. The physical space should allow its (7)_____ to function as efficiently and comfortably as possible.

Although form *and* function is obviously the ideal, it is not always so easy to achieve, as shortcomings in several (8)_____ buildings have shown.

5 UNDERSTANDING PARAPHRASE **Write the number of the original sentences from the essay next to the paraphrases below.**

Original sentences

1 Beautiful, well-constructed buildings are a symbol of a civilized society.

2 People say that living or working in an ugly place creates a depressing and uninspiring environment.

3 Many people believe that architects have a wider responsibility to society than just designing functional buildings.

4 "Less is more."

5 It seems that even these two celebrated designs have problems with functionality.

6 Each type of building has a different function, and, therefore, it has a different form.

Paraphrases

_____ a Unattractive buildings can make people feel unhappy and bored.

_____ b Attractive, safe buildings represent a cultured society.

_____ c A minimalist design can actually create a more powerful effect.

_____ d Every construction has a different purpose, and is therefore designed according to different criteria.

_____ e These famous buildings may have won awards, but they still do not always fulfill users' needs.

_____ f People who design buildings have a duty to the general public.

READING BETWEEN THE LINES

6 MAKING INFERENCES   **Work with a partner. Discuss the questions.**

1   Why are well-designed buildings advantageous for the owner?

2   Why is a circular or "satellite" shape beneficial for an airport terminal?

3   Why might governments demolish ugly public buildings?

4   What elements of a building could make it depressing?

5   Why could the design of a building increase your motivation?

☼ CRITICAL THINKING

7 SYNTHESIZING   **Work with a partner. Use ideas from Reading 1 and Reading 2 to discuss the questions.**

APPLY	ANALYZE	EVALUATE
How would you design your own home if you didn't have to be concerned about the cost?	Which is more important: a home that is eco-friendly, or one that is beautiful to look at? Why?	Do you agree that architects have a wider responsibility to society, or should they just do what their clients want? Why?

⚙ COLLABORATION

8 A   Work in a small group. Brainstorm at least five advantages of beautiful buildings and five advantages of functional buildings in the T-chart.

beauty	function

B   As a class, think of at least 10 buildings and write them on the board.

C   Use your group's T-chart to evaluate each building. Decide if each one is more beautiful or more functional. Compare your answers with the rest of the class.

LANGUAGE DEVELOPMENT

ACADEMIC WORD FAMILIES

1 **Complete the word families in the table.**

noun	verb	adjective	adverb
function, functionalism	function	functional	functionally
environment		(1)_____	(2)_____
(3)_____	(4)_____	depressing	(5)_____
responsibility		(6)_____	(7)_____
architect, (8)_____		(9)_____	(10)_____
(11)_____		(12)_____	efficiently

2 **Complete the sentences with words from the table in Exercise 1.**

1 It is important to consider the _____ impact of any new building on its natural surroundings.

2 _____ is an architectural philosophy that believes that function is more important than beauty.

3 Environmentally friendly buildings usually use energy very _____.

4 Architects need to plan buildings _____ in order to ensure that they are sustainable.

5 Badly designed buildings can _____ even the happiest person.

6 One famous critic described _____ as "frozen music," meaning the design of a building is artistic.

7 Architects must consider the impact of buildings on the _____.

8 Employers must be _____ for providing safe working areas.

ARCHITECTURE AND PLANNING VOCABULARY

3 Complete the definitions with the words from the box. Use a dictionary or the Internet to help you.

| amenities | green belt | outskirts | skyscrapers |
| structural engineer | suburban | urban sprawl |

1 A person who has special training that enables him or her to help build an architectural design is a _____ .

2 _____ are very tall modern buildings in cities.

3 When cities spread out into the countryside, and parking lots or new buildings replace forests and fields, the result is called _____ .

4 A _____ is a section of nature in or near a city that cannot be developed or built on.

5 _____ neighborhoods are not located within a city. They are found on the _____ of a city and usually have houses rather than apartment buildings.

6 Public _____ are facilities that people enjoy living near, such as libraries, swimming pools, and playgrounds.

4 Complete the sentences with your own ideas.

1 The key responsibility of an architect is _____

_____ .

2 When building skyscrapers, it is important to _____

_____ .

3 Conservation may be expensive, but _____

_____ .

4 Green belt land is important because _____

_____ .

5 Important amenities that should be provided by the government include _____

_____ .

6 Urban sprawl has a negative effect on the environment because

_____ .

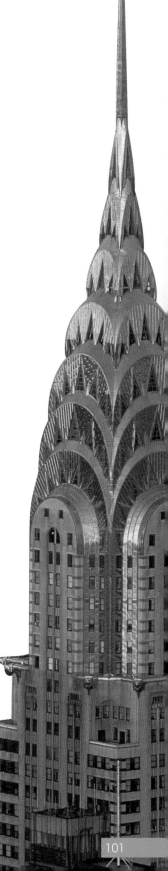

WATCH AND LISTEN

AC (n)   air conditioner; a machine that keeps the air cool in a building or car

upgrade (n)   an improvement of something so that it is more efficient, of a higher quality, or a newer model

jump on the bandwagon (idm)   to join an already successful activity or popular trend

foreclose (v)   to take control of an owner's property for not paying back the loan used to buy it

renovate (v)   to repair and improve a building

commute (v)   to travel regularly between home and work or school

PREPARING TO WATCH

1 ACTIVATING YOUR KNOWLEDGE **Work with a partner. Make a list of five things to consider when you buy a home. Put them in order of importance. Compare your answers with another pair.**

2 PREDICTING CONTENT USING VISUALS **Look at the pictures from the video. Discuss the questions with your partner.**

1   What is the man in the second picture doing?

2   Look at the houses in the pictures. How are they the same? How are they different?

3   How do you think the last picture is connected to the others?

WHILE WATCHING

3 UNDERSTANDING MAIN IDEAS **Watch the video. Circle the correct answer.**

1   What changes has Dan Sharp made to his home?

   a   added solar panels, solar lighting, and green space

   b   added solar panels and green space, and removed the AC

   c   added solar panels and solar lighting, and removed the AC

2 What is the most important to homeowners when looking at green homes?

   a the price of the home

   b solar power

   c energy efficiency

3 Which statement best summarizes how most people feel about building and living in energy-efficient homes?

   a It is necessary to preserve our planet.

   b Most people are willing to pay a little more if it saves them money in the long term.

   c Most people are unwilling to pay a little more, even if it saves them money in the long term.

4 SUMMARIZING **Watch again. Complete the summary with the missing numbers.**

> The Sharps' electric bill used to be between (1) $_____ and (2) $_____ a year. It is now (3) $_____. Like the Sharps, more people are going greener. In a survey, (4) _____% of responders said that they took steps last year to make their homes greener. However, (5) _____% of them took those steps to save money rather than to protect the environment. One example of a green home community is outside Los Angeles. Every month, homeowners could save up to (6) $_____ on their utility bills. Another community in Phoenix is selling energy-efficient homes for as little as (7) $_____.

☼ CRITICAL THINKING

5 **Work in a small group. Discuss the questions.**

APPLY	ANALYZE	EVALUATE
How is your home, school, or office green? How could it be greener?	What would persuade you to buy an energy-efficient home?	Is it better to buy a new house or renovate an old one? Explain your answer.

☺ COLLABORATION

6 **A** Work with a partner. Make a list of 10 things to consider when buying or renting a home. Rank them in order of importance to you.

    B Do a survey. Ask at least five people to rank your list in order of importance. Add any new ideas they have to your list. Then summarize the results of your survey and present them to the class.

ENERGY

LEARNING OBJECTIVES

Key Reading Skill	Working out meaning from context
Additional Reading Skills	Predicting content using visuals; understanding key vocabulary; reading for main ideas; reading for details; using your knowledge; taking notes; making inferences; synthesizing
Language Development	Energy collocations; formal and informal academic verbs

ACTIVATE YOUR KNOWLEDGE

Work with a partner. Discuss the questions.

1 Look at the photo. What kind of energy is being created here?

2 What are fossil fuels? What is renewable energy?

3 Would you be willing to pay a much higher bill if the energy company invested in solar or wind energy? Why or why not?

4 Is it a good idea to rely on energy from other countries?

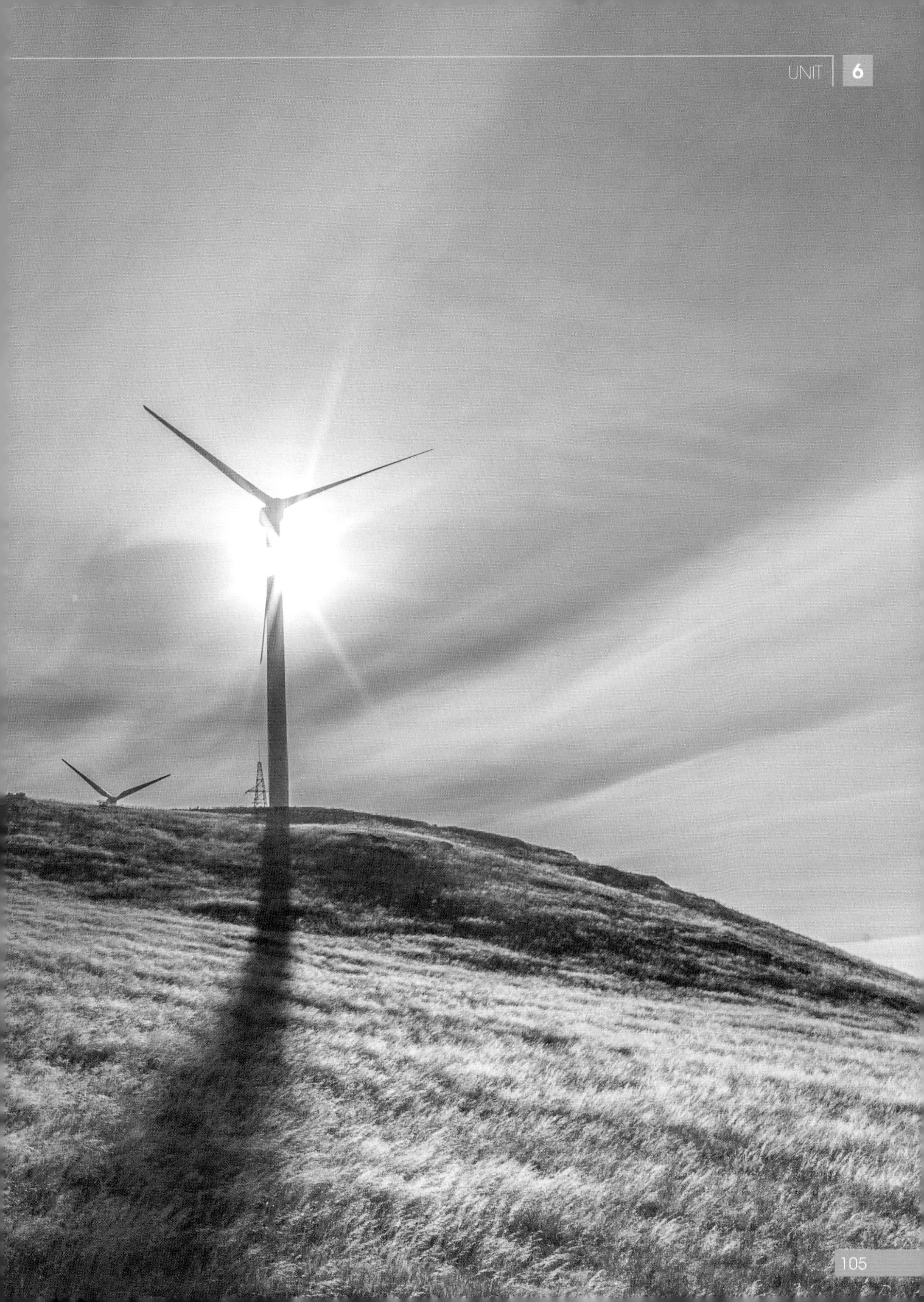

PREPARING TO READ

1 PREDICTING CONTENT USING VISUALS **Work with a partner. Look at the photos. Match the types of renewable energy in the box to the correct photo.**

> biomass energy   geothermal energy   hydropower
>
> solar power   wind power

1 _____

2 _____

3 _____

4 _____

5 _____

2 UNDERSTANDING KEY VOCABULARY **Read the sentences and write the words in bold next to the definitions.**

1 **Aquatic** creatures include fish, dolphins, and whales.

2 Oil companies often drill **offshore** to get petroleum from the sea floor.

3 Energy from the sun is considered an **inexhaustible** resource; as long as the sun is there, it can give us energy.

4 The **initial** response to the recycling program has been good. Now let's see what happens next.

5 Waterfalls **generate** energy that we can use as power.

6 All countries around the world need energy sources for their cars, machines, and appliances. This need is **universal**.

7 Many people think that we need to **utilize** existing renewable energy sources such as solar and wind power.

a _____ (adj) at the beginning; first

b _____ (v) to cause to exist; produce

c _____ (adj) living in, happening in, or connected with water

d _____ (adv) away from or at a distance from the land

e _____ (adj) existing everywhere or involving everyone

f _____ (v) to make use of something

g _____ (adj) in such large amounts that it cannot be used up

HYDROPOWER

1 Hydropower is created when moving water turns turbines to create electricity. The source of the moving water can be rivers, waterfalls, or the sea. Because flowing water continues to move, this creates an **inexhaustible** amount of energy that can be stored and used when the demand is highest. There are a few drawbacks, however. Water-powered turbines can have a negative environmental impact on **aquatic** wildlife and can endanger boats. Also, creating hydropower dams causes land behind the dams to permanently flood. Finally, it is expensive to set up hydropower systems—the average cost is between $1 million and $4 million.

WIND POWER

2 To create wind power, large turbines are placed on top of hills or **offshore**. The wind turns the blades, which **generate** energy. Wind turbines can be **utilized** on a large scale or on a small scale. Unlike hydropower, this process is relatively cheap and is considered one of the most affordable forms of electricity today. Also, it does not harm the air or land it uses. However, many people consider wind turbines ugly and noisy. Also, they rely on the wind, so if it is not windy, no energy is produced. Finally, like hydropower, wind turbines can be a threat to wildlife such as local birds.

SOLAR ENERGY

3 To use solar energy, solar panels absorb sunlight and, using devices called *photovolta*. *cells*, turn it into electricity. The sun produces energy constantly, which makes solar energy inexhaustible resource. Another benefit is tha it generates no pollution. Solar energy can be adapted to work on a variety of buildings and a variety of environments. However, a large a of land is needed to produce a large amount o solar power. Scientists have determined that we wanted to try to power the entire Earth wi renewable solar power, we would need to cov a land area about the size of Spain with solar panels. In places with less sunlight, solar pow generation has limitations. Also, photovoltaic cells are fragile and can be easily damaged.

BIOMASS ENERGY

4 Biomass is a biologically produced fuel made from plant and animal material, which is mostly composed of carbon, hydrogen, and oxygen. It is the oldest source of renewable energy, used since humans first started burning wood for fire. Today, steam from burning biomass—made up of trash and other organic waste, rather than wood—turns turbines, generating electricity. Biomass can re-grow over a relatively short period of time compared to the hundreds of millions of years that it takes for fossil fuels to form. It is also an efficient way to generate power, and it is **universal**. Another benefit is that it reduces the need to bury garbage under the ground in a landfill. However, some people are concerned that burning biomass contributes to global warming because it produces greenhouse gases[1]. Also, using biomass to generate energy on a large scale can be expensive.

Geothermal Regions of the World

GEOTHERMAL ENERGY

5 With geothermal energy, heat that is trapped in the ground can be converted into steam to turn turbines. The power it generates can then be used to produce electricity and heat buildings. Geothermal energy uses relatively simple technology. Like several of the other energy sources already mentioned, this process causes no pollution and is inexhaustible. The most active geothermal resources are usually found in areas near volcanoes or where geothermal activity naturally occurs. The largest area of this kind is known as the "Ring of Fire." It rims the Pacific Ocean and is bounded by eastern Asia and the western edge of the Americas. Outside of regions like these, geothermal energy is usually unavailable. The **initial** costs of installing a geothermal energy system are very high, but once it is built, the running costs are low.

[1]greenhouse gases (n) gases, such as carbon dioxide, that cause a gradual warming of the Earth's atmosphere

3 READING FOR MAIN IDEAS **Read the fact sheet on pages 108–109 and choose the best title.**

a   "Why Are Fossil Fuels Running Out?"

b   "The Disadvantages of Clean Energy Generation"

c   "An Overview of Renewable Energy Production"

d   "The Benefits of Renewable Energy Sources"

e   "The Pros and Cons of Environmental Conservation"

4 READING FOR DETAILS **Read the fact sheet again. Which types of renewable energy do the sentences describe? Write the correct type next to each sentence.**

1   This source of energy can be used for many purposes and will last forever, but it cannot work 24 hours a day. _____

2   This type of energy produces greenhouse gases, but disposes of waste.

_____

3   This type of energy which is based on steam-powered turbines is expensive to set up but cheap to operate. _____

4   This type of energy may require some people to relocate.

_____

5   This type of energy may be more common or relevant in countries that have deserts or are near the equator. _____

6   This type of energy is expensive to begin with, although the technology is relatively basic. _____

5 Match each newspaper headline to a renewable energy source. Write the correct type of energy next to each headline.

1   "Wave-power Machines Struggle in Marine Environment"

_____

2   "Rare Eagle Struck by Newly Constructed Turbine" _____

3   "Report Shows 11 Tons (10,000 kg) of Waste Used Last Year to Fuel Energy Plant" _____

4   "Amazing Summer Weather Creates a Huge Supply of Energy"

_____

5   "Government Pledges Millions for New Plant Near Volcano"

_____

6   "Low Rainfall Suggests High Electricity Prices" _____

7   "Environmentalists Question the Ability of this Bio-energy Source to Renew Itself" _____

READING BETWEEN THE LINES

⚒ SKILLS

WORKING OUT MEANING FROM CONTEXT

When you read a word you do not understand in a text, try to guess its meaning from the context before using a dictionary. Often you do not need the exact meaning of the word to be able to understand the sentence. To guess the meaning of an unknown word, look at the words before and after it. Look for clues to the meaning.

- Can you use logic and your knowledge of the world to guess?

  Days without sun are **rare** in the desert.

- Is the word explained in the text or are examples given?

  The nest of an **eagle**, one of the world's largest hunting birds, was destroyed when the company built the power station.

- Do linking words or conjunctions help you guess?

  Although the government has **pledged** to build a new wind farm, some believe this will not happen.

6 WORKING OUT MEANING **Read the fact sheet again and find the following words. Identify their meaning. Highlight the words that helped you guess the meaning.**

1	solar	4	geothermal
2	fragile	5	wildlife
3	stored	6	bury

☀ CRITICAL THINKING

7 **Work with a partner. Discuss the questions.**

APPLY

What renewable energy sources are used in your city or country?

ANALYZE

Nuclear power is also an alternative to fossil fuels. What are the problems with nuclear power?

EVALUATE

What is more important: the cost or the environmental impact of energy use? Why?

⚇ COLLABORATION

8 A Work in a small group. Brainstorm a list of all the energy sources you know.

B Compare your list with another group. Add any new sources to your list.

C Choose an alternative energy source that is not in Reading 1. Research the energy source. Write a paragraph with visuals to add to the fact sheet in Reading 1. Share it with the class.

READING 2

PREPARING TO READ

1 **Read the definitions. Complete the sentences with the correct form of the words in bold.**

> **address** (v)   to give attention to or to deal with a matter or problem
>
> **adopt** (v)   to accept or begin to use something
>
> **alarming** (adj)   causing worry or fear
>
> **diminish** (v)   to reduce or be reduced in size or importance
>
> **instigate** (v)   to cause an event or situation to happen
>
> **resistant** (adj)   not accepting of something
>
> **urgent** (adj)   needing immediate attention
>
> **vital** (adj)   necessary or extremely important for the success or continued existence of something

1 Environmentalists feel that finding solutions to fight climate change is a(n) _____ issue and needs to be addressed right now.

2 Some people find global warming _____ because the future of planet Earth could be in danger.

3 The government plans to _____ a recycling program similar to the one Germany has and is also looking into building wind power turbines.

4 Over one hundred United Nations delegates signed a document to _____ climate change and establish new environmental standards.

5 The aim of this plan is to _____ pollution to lower levels.

6 Many people say it is _____ for the survival of certain plant and animal species that we stop pollution caused by factories.

7   Manufacturers may be _____ to using more "green" production methods, so we need new laws that force them to do it.

8   The 1962 book *Silent Spring* by Rachel Carson _____ the modern environmental movement.

2 USING YOUR KNOWLEDGE   **What will happen when the world starts to run out of these resources?**

1   oil *prices will rise; gasoline will be more expensive* _____

2   water _____

3   trees _____

4   food _____

5   metal _____

3 How can people tackle the problem of resource shortages?

1   oil *invest in renewable resources like wind energy* _____

2   water _____

3   trees _____

4   food _____

5   metal _____

4 Work with a partner. You are going to read an essay that discusses the "Reduce, Reuse, Recycle" strategy. Discuss what you think this means. Think of examples of things you can reduce, reuse, or recycle.

5 After you read the essay, check your answers in Exercise 4.

REDUCE, REUSE, RECYCLE

WE MUST MAINTAIN OUR NATURAL RESOURCES

1 The world's natural resources are being used at an **alarming** rate—not only fossil fuels such as coal, oil, and gas, but also water, wood, metals, and minerals. This has many potential consequences for the billions of people who live on Earth. In recent years, both individuals and governments have become more interested in better managing the world's resources. While alternative energy solutions are important, they are not always feasible[1]. An immediate way to improve the situation is to encourage everyone to "reduce, reuse, recycle."

2 We must all learn to use fewer natural resources on a day-to-day basis. We can start by reducing the number of electrical items we leave plugged in, using less water, and avoiding motorized transportation. Many cities are **instigating** carbon emissions taxes, which is a step in the right direction. In our homes, we can use only energy-saving light bulbs and install water meters. Parents need to train children from an early age to turn off lights that they are not using. It is sometimes difficult to persuade people to use less energy and water, or to eat less food, but an effective way to motivate people to **adopt** less-wasteful practices is to make these essential commodities much more expensive.

3 It is often possible to restore old, unwanted objects to a state in which they can be used again. Glass bottles can be cleaned and reused without having to be broken and remade. Reusing things is a very efficient process and consumes less energy than recycling. It does, however, often require a lot of expensive organization and administration. There are also concerns to **address** regarding reused medical equipment and food-storage items, for example, because of safety and hygiene issues. Still, the benefits of reusing items are clear.

4 Most of us know that materials such as paper and plastic can be recycled into new products. This process uses less energy and emits fewer greenhouse gases than producing articles from raw materials. Yes, sorting through used materials before recycling them is a dirty and difficult job, and breaking up electronic equipment to recycle rare metals is time-consuming and potentially dangerous. But provided we understand the dangers involved, the necessity of recycling on a community scale is evident.

Bales of paper waiting to be recycled

5 A lot of attention has been paid in recent years to the dangers of relying on fossil fuels. For this reason, the use of alternatives to coal, oil, and gas are becoming more and more common. Alternative energy sources can be recovered or produced without emitting carbon dioxide and contributing to global warming. They can decrease air pollution, which is better for our health, as it **diminishes** instances of asthma[2]. They are often sustainable resources as well, which means they will not get used up.

6 There are many examples of alternative energy sources. Hydropower utilizes the power of moving water such as waterfalls and rivers. Large turbines can be used to generate wind power. Solar energy uses panels that absorb sunlight and turn it into electricity by way of photovoltaic cells. The burning of biomass can be used to create steam. Finally, geothermal energy uses the heat within the earth to produce electricity and heat buildings. A particular type of alternative energy may work the best for a particular region. The other side of this is that some of these energy sources may not be available at all to people in certain places because of environmental limitations.

7 To avoid a catastrophic[3] depletion of **vital** natural resources in the future, **urgent** action is required now. Alternative energy production is certainly essential, but it can be expensive and time-consuming to install the required elements. Some developing areas of the world may simply be unable to pay for it. In other places, corporations and taxpayers may be **resistant** to it. The "reduce, reuse, recycle" strategy, at least for the present, seems to be a manageable one that can be practiced by both individuals and organizations. People may be resistant to the idea of changing their ways or increasing the cost of their routines by "going green," but it is crucial that we do this for the future of the planet.

[1]feasible (adj) possible, reasonable, or likely
[2]asthma (n) an illness that makes it difficult to breathe
[3]catastrophic (adj) related to a sudden event that causes great suffering or destruction

6 READING FOR MAIN IDEAS **Read the essay on pages 114–115. Discuss the questions with a partner.**

1 Is the writer's point that one of the methods (reducing, reusing, or recycling) is better than the others?

2 What are some drawbacks offered for relying on alternative energy sources?

3 What is the writer's final conclusion on this topic?

7 TAKING NOTES **Look at the notes a student took while reading the essay. Find and highlight the missing information in the text. Then complete the notes.**

1 PARA 1: To better manage resources, reduce, _____, & _____

2 PARA. 2: Use fewer resources – save electricity, _____, & _____

3 PARA 3: Reuse items, e.g. glass bottles – but be careful when reusing _____ & _____

4 PARA 4: Recycling _____ = easy; recycling _____ = difficult & dangerous

5 PARA 5: Need to use more alternative energy, fewer _____

6 PARA 6: Alternative energy examples: _____, _____, _____, _____, _____

7 PARA 7: Need to _____

READING BETWEEN THE LINES

8 MAKING INFERENCES **Work with a partner. Answer the questions based on ideas in the essay.**

1 Why will energy need to become more expensive before people are motivated to reduce the energy they use?

2 Why should we avoid the use of motorized transportation?

3 Why might it be dangerous to reuse medical equipment?

4 Why might corporations that manufacture products be resistant to environmental laws?

⌀ CRITICAL THINKING

9 SYNTHESIZING **Work with a partner. Use ideas from Reading 1 and Reading 2 to discuss the questions.**

APPLY	ANALYZE	EVALUATE
Is recycling common in your country? What objects can be recycled?	Is it fair to penalize people financially if they do not recycle? Explain your reasons.	When evaluating energy sources, what is more important: their appearance and noise or their effectiveness?

⚒ COLLABORATION

10 A Work with two partners. Choose three types of renewable energy, and complete the chart.

energy type	benefits	drawbacks	effectiveness/impact

B Prepare a group presentation about renewable energy. Include an introduction, a discussion of the three types you chose, and a conclusion, with time for questions and answers at the end.

ENERGY COLLOCATIONS

1 Match the nouns in the box to the correct group of words.

| energy   fuel   pollution   problem   production   source |

1 fossil / diesel / alternative / renewable / clean _____

2 renewable / green / nuclear / solar / geothermal _____

3 environmental / air / industrial / water / radioactive _____

4 energy / fuel / power / water / renewable _____

5 electricity / energy / oil / gas / agricultural _____

6 serious / health / environmental / major / medical _____

2 Complete the sentences using energy collocations from Exercise 1.

1 Critics of _____ energy say that the risks to the environment outweigh the benefits of cheap electricity.

2 Asthma and diabetes are increasingly common _____ problems.

3 For a renewable _____ of electricity to be truly successful, governments have to invest more money in it.

4 _____ fuels, such as oil and gas, have a finite lifespan.

5 _____ energy, whichever renewable source it comes from, tends to be slightly more expensive for the user.

6 Rivers and lakes are two major _____ sources that can be used for hydroelectric power.

FORMAL AND INFORMAL ACADEMIC VERBS

3 **Match formal verbs with informal alternatives.**

1	consult	a	get
2	contest	b	skip; leave out
3	deliver	c	start
4	diminish	d	look at
5	instigate	e	use
6	omit	f	decrease
7	secure	g	give
8	utilize	h	disagree with

4 **Complete the sentences with the correct forms of the formal verbs in Exercise 3.**

1 Resources are beginning to _____; soon they will run out.

2 This company needs to _____ its energy policy to the government by the end of the year.

3 The application to construct a wind farm in this area has been _____ by local residents who dislike the idea.

4 If people _____ the documents on our website, they can see how biofuel is made.

5 The rise in fuel prices should _____ a debate on oil reserves.

6 This car _____ fuel more efficiently than previous models.

7 Advocates of biofuels sometimes _____ key details such as how much land is needed to cultivate the crops. People who disagree with them would certainly use this information to argue against biofuel advocates.

8 This country must _____ new renewable energy sources.

herd (n)   a large group of animals, such as cows, that live and eat together

hum (v)   to be very busy and full of activity

renewable energy (n)   energy that is produced using the sun, wind, etc. rather than using fuels such as oil and coal

grid (n)   a system of wires through which electricity is connected to different parts of a region

die down (phr v)   to become reduced in strength

PREPARING TO WATCH

1 ACTIVATING YOUR KNOWLEDGE **Check (✓) the statements that you agree with. Discuss your answers with a partner.**

1 ☐ We use more energy now than we did 10 years ago.
2 ☐ Energy is becoming more expensive.
3 ☐ There are many alternative energy sources.
4 ☐ Fossil fuel is our only source of energy.
5 ☐ It is not a problem to depend on only one energy source.
6 ☐ Energy from wind and the sun will become our main energy source in the future.

2 PREDICTING CONTENT USING VISUALS **Look at the pictures from the video. Discuss the questions with your partner.**

1 What parts of North America do you think use wind to produce energy?
2 How do the wind turbines in the first two pictures differ from the one in the third picture? Which ones do you think produce the most power?
3 What does "Wind Alley" refer to?

WHILE WATCHING

3 UNDERSTANDING MAIN IDEAS **Watch the video. Write *T* (true) or *F* (false) next to the statements. Correct the false statements.**

_____ 1 Jerry Tuttle is responsible for keeping the turbines operating.

_____ 2 The wind turbines in Sweetwater are responsible for producing 13% of the electricity for Texas.

_____ 3 Samuel Barr's windmill only generates enough electricity to run his coffee machine.

_____ 4 One criticism of wind turbines is that they are in locations where the most power is needed.

_____ 5 The greatest demand for electricity is in the summer, and winds are usually weaker during that time of the year.

4 UNDERSTANDING DETAILS **Watch again. Write a supporting detail for each main idea.**

1 Texas produces more electricity from wind than any other state.

_____

2 Samuel Barr split the cost of his windmill with the state of New York.

_____

3 Many states, companies, and individuals invested in new wind projects last year.

_____

4 There are some drawbacks to wind turbines.

_____

⌁ CRITICAL THINKING

5 **Work in a small group. Discuss the questions.**

APPLY	ANALYZE	EVALUATE
Would you install a personal windmill at your home? Why or why not?	Are there places in the world that would benefit from wind turbines more than others? Where are they?	Who should be responsible for the cost of installing turbines or windmills? Why?

COLLABORATION

6 **A** Work with a partner. Create a list of 10 ways you can reduce your energy use.

B Work with another group. Compare and combine your ideas.

C Repeat step B as a class, and decide on a final list. Agree on a period of time (a weekend, a week, etc.) to follow these steps, and keep a daily journal to record your progress. At the end of the time period, discuss your results as a class.

ART AND DESIGN

LEARNING OBJECTIVES

Key Reading Skill	Scanning to find information
Additional Reading Skills	Understanding key vocabulary; predicting content using visuals; reading for details; taking notes; making inferences; using your knowledge; reading for main ideas; understanding paraphrase; identifying opinions; synthesizing
Language Development	Paraphrasing; vocabulary for art and design

ACTIVATE YOUR KNOWLEDGE

Work with a partner. Discuss the questions.

1 Do you like art and design? If so, what media (e.g., painting, music, architecture, fashion) do you like?

2 Are you artistic? If so, what kinds of artistic activities do you like doing?

3 Look at the photo. Would you call this art? Why or why not?

4 Are art and design important for a country's economy? Why or why not?

PREPARING TO READ

1 UNDERSTANDING KEY VOCABULARY **Read the definitions. Complete the sentences with the correct form of the words in bold.**

> **aesthetic** (adj)   relating to the enjoyment or study of beauty, or showing great beauty
>
> **conceptual** (adj)   based on ideas or principles
>
> **contemporary** (adj)   existing or happening now
>
> **distinction** (n)   a difference between similar things
>
> **established** (adj)   generally accepted or familiar; having a long history
>
> **notion** (n)   a belief or idea
>
> **significance** (n)   importance

1   A sculpture in which the artist's main idea or message is considered more important than the technique can be called _____ art.

2   The new museum in town has a lot of _____ appeal. The exterior of the building is very beautifully designed.

3   It is common these days to prefer _____ architecture, but I like the classic, old homes in my neighborhood.

4   In art class we learned the _____ between fine art and applied art.

5   It is now well _____ that Pablo Picasso was one of the great artists of the twentieth century.

6   Art historians often explain the _____ of very famous works of art and how they may have influenced our society.

7   Many people share the _____ that the term "art" also applies to things like car and video game design.

2 PREDICTING CONTENT USING VISUALS **Read the descriptions and match the artists to the photographs of their work.**

1 **Andy Warhol:** An artist who was famous for his colorful prints of celebrities. _____

2 **Damien Hirst:** A radical British artist who famously used dead animals in his work. _____

3 **Marcel Duchamp:** An early twentieth-century French artist who changed what people thought of sculpture. _____

4 **Frank Lloyd Wright:** An American architect who focused on the role of buildings within the landscape. _____

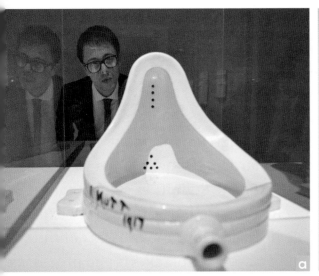

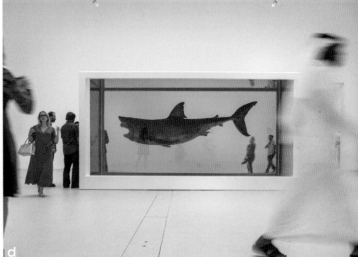

ALL THAT ART IS

1 **What is art?** This question has puzzled philosophers and great thinkers for centuries. In fact, there is disagreement about exactly what art is. Most of us would agree that Leonardo da Vinci's Mona Lisa is art, but what about a video game? One dictionary definition states that art is "making objects, images, or music, etc. that are beautiful or that express certain feelings." This, however, could be regarded as too broad a definition. There are actually a number of different categories of objects and processes under the umbrella term of art that can be explored.

---

2 Art is typically divided into two areas: fine art (such as painting, sculpture, music, and poetry) and applied art (such as pottery, weaving, metalworking, furniture making, and calligraphy). However, some claim that the art label can also be attached to car design, fashion, photography, cooking, or even sports. Fine art is categorized as something that only has an **aesthetic** or **conceptual** function. This point was made over a thousand years ago by the Greek philosopher Aristotle, who wrote, "the aim of art is to represent not the outward appearance of things but their inward **significance**." He noted that artists produced objects, drama, and music that reflected their emotions and ideas, rather than just trying to capture a true image of nature. Andy Warhol, the American artist famous for his Pop Art in the 1960s, once said, "An artist produces things that people don't need to have." This is the **distinction** between fine and applied art. Applied arts require an object to be functional as well as beautiful.

3 In the twentieth century, artists began to challenge the **established** idea of art. They recognized that their work belonged to the higher social classes who had the wealth to purchase art and the leisure time to enjoy it. The architect Frank Lloyd Wright commented, "Art for art's sake is a philosophy of the well-fed." In an attempt to challenge this **notion**, the French painter Marcel Duchamp submitted a toilet to an art exhibition in 1917 instead of a painting.

He signed it and said, "Everything an artist produces is art." Today, many people complain about the lack of skill in the production of conceptual artistic objects. Some **contemporary** artists use assistants to produce all their art for them. British artist Damien Hirst claims that as long as he had the idea, it is his work. He has compared his art to architecture, saying, "You have to look at it as if the artist is an architect, and we don't have a problem that great architects don't actually build the houses."

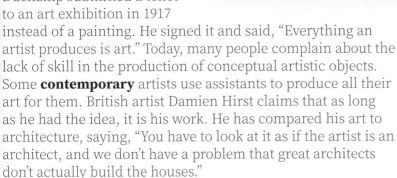

66 Everything an artist produces is art. 99

4 Despite a hundred years of modern art, fine art is still regarded as a preserve of the wealthy. Hirst's works, for example, sell for millions of dollars. Even so, we can see examples of art all around us that are not expensive. Many towns and cities have public art that can be enjoyed by all. Some museums, like the National Gallery of Art in Washington, D.C., are free. Others are free for children and students. Street art is also popular in different neighborhoods around the world. One British artist, Banksy, has become world-famous for unauthorized[1] works of art painted on building walls. These can be viewed at no charge by anyone who knows where to look.

5 Art anthropologist Ellen Dissanayake, in the book *What is Art For?* offers one intriguing function of art: "the heightening of existence." In other words, art makes our ordinary, everyday lives a little more special. This notion may not apply to all art, but perhaps we can agree that it is a good goal toward which all artists should reach.

[1]unauthorized (adj) without official permission

⚒ SKILLS

SCANNING TO FIND INFORMATION

Scanning is a reading technique used to look for specific information in a text. If you know what information you want from a text, you do not need to read it all. Just move your eye quickly down the page looking for the key words related to the information you want. When you find the information, you can just read that part in detail.

3 SCANNING TO FIND INFORMATION **Scan the article on pages 126–127, and put the artists in the order in which they are mentioned.**

a   Andy Warhol   _____

b   Damien Hirst   _____

c   Marcel Duchamp   _____

d   Frank Lloyd Wright   _____

4 READING FOR DETAILS **Read the article. Write _T_ (true), _F_ (false), or _DNS_ (does not say) next to the statements. Correct the false statements.**

_____ 1   The writer feels that the dictionary definition of art is too wide.

_____ 2   Metalworking is an example of fine art.

_____ 3   Some people argue that sports are a type of art.

_____ 4   Aristotle was the first to say that art should be affordable for all.

_____ 5   Andy Warhol invented Pop Art.

_____ 6   "Art for art's sake" refers to applied art.

_____ 7   Duchamp's toilet was sold at an art exhibition for a very high price.

_____ 8   Damien Hirst produces all his own art.

5 TAKING NOTES **Use the diagram as a model to take notes on the article. Paragraph 1 has been done for you.**

idea

many definitions

P1 topic

What is art?

subject

Art

P2 topic

idea

examples

categories of art
categories of
processes

examples

READING BETWEEN THE LINES

6 MAKING INFERENCES **Which of the artists mentioned in the article would probably have these opinions?**

1   It is the idea of the work of art that is most important.

2   Art isn't functional.

3   Everything an artist makes can be considered art.

4   A building wall can be used like a canvas.

5   It does not matter if the artist doesn't actually make the work of art.

6   Only the rich think that art does not need a purpose.

☀ CRITICAL THINKING

7 **Work with a partner. Discuss the questions.**

APPLY

Which of the artists in the text do you agree with most? Why?

ANALYZE

Do you think art is only for rich people? Why or why not?

EVALUATE

Should car design be classified as art? Why or why not?

⚙ COLLABORATION

8 A   Work in a small group. Discuss the following questions:

- What is the main purpose of art?

- Does art have to have a purpose, or can it just be beautiful or interesting to look at?

B   Choose three examples of "art for art's sake" and three examples of "art that has a purpose." Share your examples with the class, and explain your choices.

C   As a class, classify all the examples of art by category on the board.

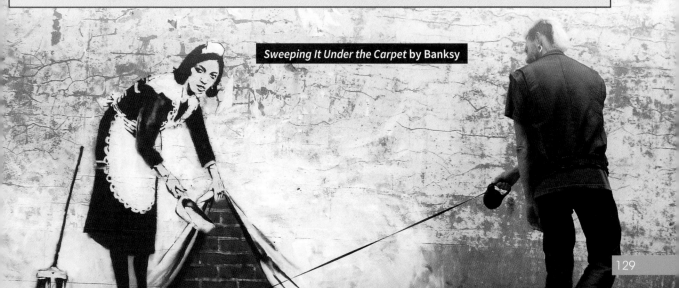

Sweeping It Under the Carpet **by Banksy**

PREPARING TO READ

1 USING YOUR KNOWLEDGE **Work with a partner. Put a check next to the activities you think are considered art. Explain your reasons.**

a ☐ computer games

b ☐ cooking

c ☐ drawing

d ☐ fashion

e ☐ football

f ☐ gardening

g ☐ photography

h ☐ sculpture

2 UNDERSTANDING KEY VOCABULARY **Read the sentences and choose the best definition for the words in bold.**

1 Critics **perceived** him to be an especially good painter of real-life situations.

a thought of in a particular way

b misunderstood

2 A camera, unlike a person's hand, is a **mechanical** device.

a related to fixing equipment

b related to machines

3 Some people think that taking a photo of a person is **analogous** to painting a portrait.

a similar; comparable

b the opposite of

4   The artist uses a **sophisticated** 3D printer to create perfectly identical plastic models of real people. The models show great detail from the wrinkles in people's faces to the folds in their clothing.

   a   basic and simple

   b   highly developed and complex

5   News reporting, unlike other kinds of writing, is expected to be **objective** and not based on someone's opinion.

   a   based on facts and reality

   b   focused on real objects

6   Although I do not think Banksy has the right to paint on buildings without permission, I do **acknowledge** that his work is very imaginative.

   a   agree; admit something is true

   b   make a guess about something

7   Her fiction is very **banal** because the plots are never exciting and the characters are unoriginal.

   a   popular; successful

   b   boring; uninteresting

8   I have a **cynical** view of modern art, and I wonder why it's considered good or why anyone would buy it.

   a   suspicious; negative

     formal; academic

PHOTOGRAPHY
as
ART

1 The production of fine art is the use of skill and imagination to create aesthetic objects or experiences that can be shared with other people....

... Photography is thought by some to be a form of fine art because it is made using the same critical and creative process that a painter or sculptor would use. It seems clear, however, that there is a significant difference between creating images by hand—using paint, clay, or other tools—and pointing a **mechanical** device at something interesting and clicking. Although photography does have some features in common with other kinds of art, it cannot be said that photography is unquestionably art.

2 It is true that photography can be appreciated on the same level as other recognized forms of visual art. Sometimes decisions involved in creating a photograph are **analogous** to those made by any other artist. A photograph is not always just a **banal** record of the world, but a deliberately created image with its own artistic features. Ansel Adams, the American photographer, commented on this point when he noted that *take* is not the right verb for a photograph. Instead, he said, one *makes* a photograph. To this end, there is a growing trend for photographers to call themselves artists. Nevertheless, we cannot ignore the fact that artists can sell their pieces in the higher-priced, fine-art markets, whereas photographers cannot. A photograph by German artist Andreas Gursky, for example, recently sold for almost $4.5 million. As **cynical** as it may sound, no one would likely pay that much for a photograph unless the photographer presented himself as an artist.

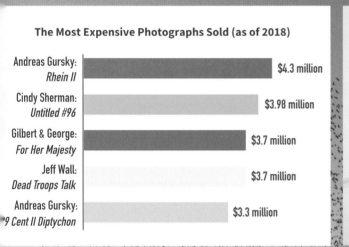

The Most Expensive Photographs Sold (as of 2018)

Andreas Gursky: *Rhein II*	$4.3 million
Cindy Sherman: *Untitled #96*	$3.98 million
Gilbert & George: *For Her Majesty*	$3.7 million
Jeff Wall: *Dead Troops Talk*	$3.7 million
Andreas Gursky: *9 Cent II Diptychon*	$3.3 million

3 In truth, most photographs are basically **objective** records of a particular place at a particular time. Certainly we can appreciate a beautiful photograph when we see one, but any beauty that is **perceived** in the picture comes from the time and place where it was taken, and it is not the creation of the photographer. Also, **sophisticated** and expensive equipment often plays a greater role in the success of a photograph than the photographer's creativity. Even some of the greatest photographers **acknowledge** that there is a limit to the amount of influence they can have on a final product. Henri Cartier-Bresson, the famous French photographer, admitted that luck was the most important factor. Finally, photography is so widely used for practical functions that have little or nothing to do with art, such as police work, advertising, and news reporting, that it cannot claim to be made for aesthetic purposes alone.

4 People have argued whether photography is art ever since the first photographers shared their work. A photographer may make the same aesthetic choices as a fine artist: subject matter, lighting, color, or even a theme or message. However, cameras can also be purely functional tools, capturing visual records and presenting information. Photography is a medium that can be used to make art, but that does not mean that all photography is art.

WHILE READING

3 READING FOR MAIN IDEAS **Read the essay on pages 132–133. In which paragraphs are these points discussed?**

1   The concept that fine art is one thing and photography is another.   _____

2   Photography is more objective than other kinds of art.   _____

3   Some photographers are more vocal about calling themselves artists.   _____

4   Photography is a means of producing art, but it's not always art.   _____

READING BETWEEN THE LINES

4 MAKING INFERENCES **Read the essay. Answer the questions.**

1   Which statement would the author of the article agree with most?

  a   Photography is never art.

  b   Photography shares some things in common with other art forms.

2   Why does the author mention the high selling price of the Andreas Gursky photograph?

  a   to imply that photographers may call themselves artists to make more money

  b   to show that even if it is not art, photographs are valuable

3   Why does the author paraphrase Henri Cartier-Bresson?

  a   because it indirectly supports the thesis

  b   to show that some photographers disagree with him

5 UNDERSTANDING PARAPHRASE **Match the paraphrases to the original statements.**

Original statements

1   … any beauty that is perceived in the picture is the beauty of the time and place where it was taken, and it is not the creation of the photographer.   _____

2   … there is a significant difference between creating images by hand—using paint, clay, or other tools—and pointing a mechanical device at something interesting and clicking.   _____

3   … photography is so widely used for practical functions that have little or nothing to do with art, such as police work, advertising, and news reporting, that it cannot claim to be made for aesthetic purposes alone.   _____

4   … he noted that *take* is not the right verb for a photograph. Instead, he said, one *makes* a photograph.   _____

Paraphrases

a   Since photography is frequently used for non-artistic purposes, it cannot be considered art.

b   Art cannot be created by a machine.

c   The aesthetic value of a photograph comes from the natural world, not from the skill of the person holding the camera.

d   Photography requires artistic input.

6 IDENTIFYING OPINIONS **Match the opinions to the people.**

Opinions

1 There's no reason for a great photograph to be any cheaper than a great painting. _____

2 Even a child could take a great picture of that view. _____

3 There's a lot more skill to making a picture than just pointing a camera at something and clicking. It's something that I create. _____

4 Most of us would just walk by and not notice something that could make a fabulous photo. And even if we did notice we probably wouldn't know how to take a photo that would stir other people's feelings. _____

5 Sometimes you just see something that will make a great picture and the light is perfect and you have your camera with you. At other times, nothing seems to be right. _____

People

a Ansel Adams

b Henri Cartier-Bresson

c Andreas Gursky

d The author of the essay

e Someone who believes photography is art

CRITICAL THINKING

7 SYNTHESIZING **Work with a partner. Use ideas from Reading 1 and Reading 2 to discuss the questions.**

APPLY

Have you ever taken an artistic photograph? Describe it.

APPLY

Do you agree with the author's thesis "It cannot be said that photography is unquestionably art"?

ANALYZE

Can a photograph really be worth $4.5 million? Why or why not?

COLLABORATION

8 A Work with a partner. Do you think photographs can achieve the level of "heightening our existence"? Write your opinions and reasons in the chart.

Yes	No	Why or why not?

B Survey five people, and add their information to the chart. Report your findings to the class.

PARAPHRASING

LANGUAGE

Writers often refer to what somebody else has written to support their arguments. One way of doing this is *paraphrasing*. Paraphrasing uses reported speech—explaining someone else's opinion without using the same words.

Henri Cartier-Bresson, the famous French photographer, admitted that luck was the most important factor.

Since the writer is not quoting the original source, it is important to make sure that the paraphrase is different from the original source (even if the main idea is the same).

Writers do this by using synonyms or antonyms, changing some of the parts of speech, or sequencing the ideas differently. Also, when attributing the idea to the original person, they use reporting verbs such as *state, say, feel, insist, believe, point out, emphasize, maintain, deny, suggest,* and *theorize.*

Notice how all of these strategies are used in the paraphrase below.

Original quote: "The chief enemy of creativity is 'good' sense." —Pablo Picasso

Paraphrase: Pablo Picasso felt that doing things in the usual, sensible way was the main obstacle to imaginative art.

1. **Read the quotations and complete the paraphrases with a reporting verb. Put the verb in the correct form.**

   1 "It is absolutely essential that children study art at school." (school superintendent)
   The superintendent _____ that art should be part of the school curriculum.

   2 "Perhaps the statue could be put in the main square." (sculptor)
   The sculptor _____ that the main square would be a suitable location for the statue.

   3 "We cannot say art is only for the wealthy because many great artists never knew anything but poverty throughout their lives." (lecturer)
   The lecturer _____ that it was not unusual for famous artists to live in poverty.

   4 "I told you. I did not steal the painting." (burglar)
   The burglar _____ that he had stolen the painting.

2. **Read the quotations and write sentences paraphrasing them. Your paraphrase should include the suggested language.**

   "A picture is worth a thousand words." —Napoleon Bonaparte (use the verb *explain*)

   Napoleon Bonaparte explained that a picture could tell us the same as a thousand words could.

1   "A picture is a poem without words." —Horace
    (use the reporting verb *pointed out* and a synonym phrase for *poem*)

    _____

2   "Creativity takes courage." —Henri Matisse
    (use the reporting verb *felt* and an antonym for *courage*)

    _____

3   "The painter has the universe in his mind and hands." —Leonardo da Vinci
    (use the reporting verb *state*, and sequence the ideas differently)

    _____

VOCABULARY FOR ART AND DESIGN

3 Read the definitions. Complete the sentences with the best adjective.

> **abstract** (adj)   relating to ideas, not physical things
>
> **avant-garde** (adj)   relating to ideas and styles that are very original and modern
>
> **decorative** (adj)   made to look attractive
>
> **expressive** (adj)   showing what somebody thinks or feels
>
> **figurative** (adj)   showing people or things in a similar way to real life
>
> **lifelike** (adj)   looks very real
>
> **monumental** (adj)   very big
>
> **moving** (adj)   causing strong feelings of sadness or sympathy

1   The _____ bronze sculpture weighs seven tons.

2   It was a(n) _____ performance that left many
    people in tears.

3   I think art is purely _____ . It is only there
    to look nice.

4   The tiger sculpture was so _____ that people
    were a little scared by it.

5   Her work was very _____ ; her ideas took
    years for people to accept as normal.

6   _____ art can look easy to produce because
    there are no realistic images.

7   He was interested in _____ art and produced
    many realistic portraits of people.

8   The paint was applied quickly to the picture in a(n) _____
    and emotional way.

a figurative drawing

WATCH AND LISTEN

leftovers (n)   food that has not been used or eaten and is kept after a meal

stall (n)   a table at a market where goods are sold

go off (phr v)   (informal, British) to spoil or rot; to go bad

tarragon (n)   a plant whose narrow leaves taste similar to licorice and are used in cooking as an herb

radish (n)   a small, round vegetable, usually red or white, that is often eaten raw in salads

tarnished (adj)   dull or discolored

capture (v)   to describe something successfully using words or pictures

PREPARING TO WATCH

1 ACTIVATING YOUR KNOWLEDGE **Work with a partner. Discuss the questions.**

1   What kinds of art do you like?

2   What materials are commonly used in art?

3   What are some nontraditional materials used in art?

2 PREDICTING CONTENT USING VISUALS **Look at the pictures from the video. Discuss the questions with your partner.**

1   What materials is the artist using?

2   Do you consider this art? Why or why not?

WHILE WATCHING

3 UNDERSTANDING MAIN IDEAS **Watch the video. Put the activities in the order that they happen (1–6).**

a   Lauren photographs her finished artwork.   _____

b   Lauren peels the skin off a radish.   _____

c   Lauren creates petals from the inside of a radish.   _____

d   Lauren finds leftovers in her refrigerator.   _____

e   Lauren arranges her design on a plate.   _____

f   Lauren thinks about what she would like to create.   _____

4 UNDERSTANDING DETAILS **Watch again. Write a supporting detail for each main idea.**

1   Lauren's work is very popular on social media.

   _____

2   There are several great food markets and stalls right outside her apartment.

   _____

3   Leftovers are used for her artwork.

   _____

4   The time of day when the piece is photographed is critical.

   _____

5 MAKING INFERENCES **Work with a partner. Discuss the questions and give reasons for your answers.**

1   Why do you think Lauren has so many followers on social media?

2   How long do you think it takes Lauren to create each piece?

3   What characteristics do you think Lauren possesses?

⌕ CRITICAL THINKING

6 **Work with a partner. Discuss the questions.**

APPLY	APPLY	ANALYZE
Do you like Lauren's work? Why or why not?	What other art have you seen that uses old materials in a creative way?	What are the benefits of using old or tarnished materials?

⚌ COLLABORATION

7 **A** Some people consider fashion, cooking, video games, and graffiti as fine art. Choose one of these or another controversial art form. Brainstorm a list of reasons why it should be considered as fine art.

   B Find one or two classmates who chose the same art form. Discuss your reasons.

   C Research the art form you chose. As a group, prepare a script for a two-minute video. Include your best arguments, and show examples of the art form. Record and/or perform the script for the class.

UNIT 8

AGING

Key Reading Skill	Using your knowledge to predict content
Additional Reading Skills	Understanding key vocabulary; reading for details; making inferences; taking notes on main ideas; scanning to find information; working out meaning; synthesizing
Language development	Academic collocations with prepositions; language of prediction

ACTIVATE YOUR KNOWLEDGE

Work with a partner. Discuss the questions below.

1 Are elderly people generally respected in your culture? Why or why not?

2 How is respect or disrespect shown to elderly people in your culture?

3 Has the perception of elderly people in your culture changed over time? In what ways?

4 Look at the photo. What do people do after they stop working in your culture?

PREPARING TO READ

1 UNDERSTANDING KEY VOCABULARY **Read the sentences and write the words in bold next to the definitions.**

1 Social scientists use **demographic** information to understand more about the populations of cities.

2 It is sometimes more difficult for older people to **adapt** to fast changing technology than it is for younger people.

3 You should ask someone else for help because I don't have time to **undertake** a new project right now.

4 In her **capacity** as head of the hospital, she makes many decisions about the budget and the staff.

5 At my school, some activities are required for all students, but others are **voluntary**.

6 In my **leisure** time, I enjoy working in my garden.

a _____ (n) a particular position or job; a role

b _____ (adj) relating to human populations and the information collected about them such as their size, growth, ages, and education

c _____ (n) the time when you are not working or doing other duties

d _____ (adj) done without being forced or paid to do it

e _____ (v) to adjust to different conditions or uses

f _____ (v) to take responsibility for and begin doing something

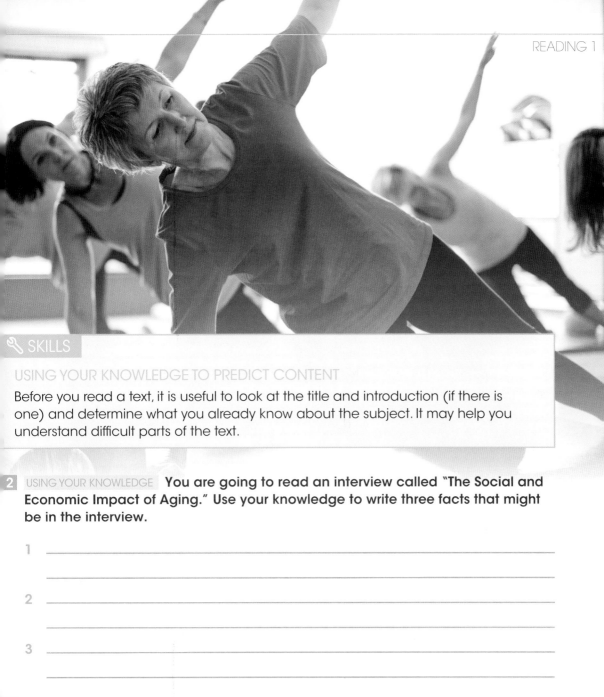

USING YOUR KNOWLEDGE TO PREDICT CONTENT

Before you read a text, it is useful to look at the title and introduction (if there is one) and determine what you already know about the subject. It may help you understand difficult parts of the text.

2   USING YOUR KNOWLEDGE   **You are going to read an interview called "The Social and Economic Impact of Aging." Use your knowledge to write three facts that might be in the interview.**

1 _____

  _____

2 _____

  _____

3 _____

  _____

3   **Work with a partner to predict the answers to the questions.**

1   Has health care throughout the world improved over the last 50 years?

2   Are people living longer or dying earlier?

3   What kinds of problems might old people face?

4   What kinds of problems might a society face if it has more elderly people?

5   What kinds of benefits can an older population bring to society?

4   **After you read the interview on pages 144–145, check your ideas in Exercise 3. If your ideas were different, why do you think that is?**

THE SOCIAL
and ECONOMIC
IMPACT OF AGING

In the next installment of our series on **demographic** changes, we interview Professor Robert Huffenheimer, an expert on the phenomenon of aging.

What exactly does *aging* mean?

It means the population in many countries is, on average, getting older. Incredibly, in the last 50 years, average life expectancy in wealthier countries has increased by half, and this trend is expected to continue.

What impact is this aging process likely to have globally?

Well, obviously it is a good thing that people are living longer, but as a result of these changes, there are a number of issues that have to be dealt with.

For example?

In certain countries, an increasing number of older people are living by themselves, often without any relatives living nearby. Some older people are simply unable to take care of themselves, and others can only do so if their houses are specially **adapted**. Likewise, they may be unable to go shopping or wash themselves, and so they need someone, perhaps a professional, to help. And, of course, older people need social activities as well.

And how are societies adapting to this?

Supermarkets, for example, have introduced more home-delivery services, which have been particularly beneficial for older people. In addition, there has been significant growth in companies providing services that would traditionally have been **undertaken** by relatives. This includes private nursing care and "meals-on-wheels" services, which deliver food to your door.

Are there any other areas where the impact of aging can be clearly seen?

Although it is not a problem yet, many governments are worried about the economic impact of an aging population. With fewer people working and paying taxes, it is obvious that governments will have less money to pay for things like health and education.

What advantages can an older population bring?

In countries where the percentage of children is lower, there are fewer education costs. In more developed countries, older people tend to have more savings and more **leisure** time. They might spend time online, or travel, or even go back to school. Of course, older people do have a lot of experience, and if they can, some continue working in a **voluntary capacity** after they retire[1]. This kind of activity adds a lot to society.

> [1] **retire** (v) to leave your job or stop working because of having reached a particular age

5 READING FOR DETAILS **Read the interview on pages 144–145. Write *T* (true), *F* (false), or *DNS* (does not say) next to the statements. Then correct the false statements.**

_____ 1 Robert Huffenheimer teaches at Columbia University.

_____ 2 The average age of the world's population has increased significantly over the last 50 years.

_____ 3 Most older people have relatives nearby.

_____ 4 There are both benefits and disadvantages for societies with aging populations.

_____ 5 So far, most private companies have ignored the changing demographic situation.

_____ 6 Most countries with an older population have much higher education costs.

_____ 7 On average, older people spend four hours per day online.

_____ 8 Countries can benefit from the skills of retired people.

6 Complete the sentences using words from the interview.

1 Specially adapted houses help elderly people who can't _____ _____ _____ themselves.

2 Older people require _____ _____ as well as professional help with shopping and washing.

3 Home deliveries and _____ _____ _____ are commercial services provided for the elderly.

4 Governments are concerned by the _____ _____ of a large number of elderly people in the population who are not working.

5 Older people are free to travel and learn new skills because they have more _____ and _____ _____.

6 Experienced older people may choose to do work on a _____ basis to help society.

READING BETWEEN THE LINES

7 MAKING INFERENCES **Work with a partner. Discuss reasons for each statement.**

1 Life expectancy increases dramatically.

2 Older people are living further away from their relatives.

3 Supermarkets have started selling groceries online.

4 Older people want to get more education.

☀ CRITICAL THINKING

8 **Work with a partner. Discuss the questions.**

APPLY	ANALYZE	EVALUATE
Does your country have a relatively young population or does it have an aging population?	What problems do elderly people in your community face?	What do you think can be done to ensure that elderly people in society are protected and cared for?

🐝 COLLABORATION

9 **A** Work with a partner. Look at the population graph for Japan and describe population trends in Japan. Discuss:
- age of data
- number of people over/under 65
- current population
- future population trends

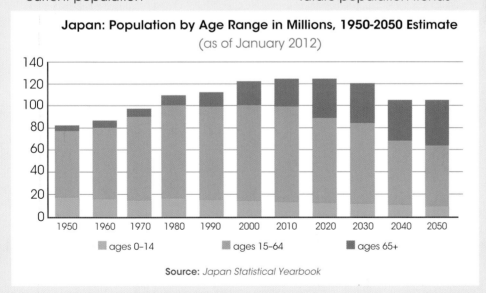

Japan: Population by Age Range in Millions, 1950-2050 Estimate
(as of January 2012)

■ ages 0–14   ■ ages 15–64   ■ ages 65+

Source: *Japan Statistical Yearbook*

B As a class, share your ideas. Make a list on the board of 5–10 possible effects on Japan if the 2050 projections are correct.

PREPARING TO READ

1 USING YOUR KNOWLEDGE **Work with a partner. Discuss the following question.**

Some countries have a higher percentage of young people than older people. What problems, impacts, and solutions might result from this?

Write about three or more countries in the chart.

country	problem	effect/impact	solution

2 UNDERSTANDING KEY VOCABULARY **Read the sentences and choose the best definition for the words in bold.**

1 In the 1800s, life expectancy was not as well-**documented** as it is today.

   a recorded or written down

   b balanced or evened out

   c understood or learned

2 The **median** age in our country is just 22, so our population is young.

   a age at which people are considered to be "middle-aged"

   b the middle number or amount in a series

   c age at which people legally become adults

3 Governments should **allocate** special funds to help elderly people pay for health care costs.

   a give something as a share of a total amount

   b make a decision about something

   c take away

4 This chart shows the **proportion** of people between the ages of 50 and 65 in the United States.

   a total number of something

   b part or share of the whole

   c advantage of something

5 In our country, a senior citizen is a person whose age falls in the **range** between age 65 and end of life.

   a area of protected land

   b section of the government

   c amount or number between a lower and upper limit

6 It can be difficult for elderly people to **cope** with the health problems of aging by themselves, so they often need special assistance.

   a deal with problems or difficulties successfully

   b make a complaint about something

   c pay for a service

7 My grandfather receives a monthly **pension** from the company that he used to work for.

   a letter with updated information

   b phone call asking for additional information

   c sum of money paid regularly to a person who has retired

Saudi Arabia:
THE REALITIES OF A YOUNG SOCIETY

1 There is a well-**documented** problem with the aging of the global population, but there are also areas of the world where demographics are very different. In many parts of the Middle East and North Africa, there is a much higher **proportion** of young people. The Kingdom of Saudi Arabia, a country of over 30 million people, is one such place. This reality has brought special challenges to the Kingdom in a number of different areas such as education, housing, and the economy.

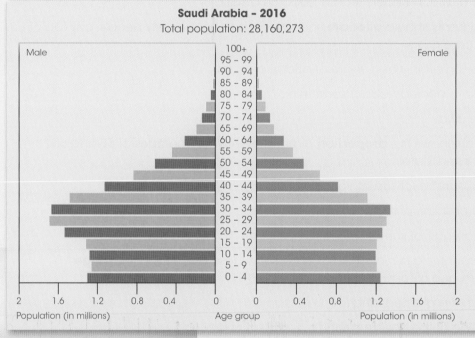

Saudi Arabia – 2016
Total population: 28,160,273

Male / Female

Age groups: 100+, 95 – 99, 90 – 94, 85 – 89, 80 – 84, 75 – 79, 70 – 74, 65 – 69, 60 – 64, 55 – 59, 50 – 54, 45 – 49, 40 – 44, 35 – 39, 30 – 34, 25 – 29, 20 – 24, 15 – 19, 10 – 14, 5 – 9, 0 – 4

Population (in millions): 2, 1.6, 1.2, 0.8, 0.4, 0

Age group

Population (in millions): 0, 0.4, 0.8, 1.2, 1.6, 2

Source: CIA, *The World Factbook*

2 The population graph shows the population of men and women in Saudi Arabia and their age **ranges** in 2016. The graph shows Saudi Arabia has a very young population. Upon close analysis, it can be seen that about 27% of the population is age 14 and under, and approximately 19% of the total population is between the ages of 15 and 24. The number of Saudis in their mid-twenties to mid-thirties is particularly high, with almost one in five of the total population falling within just this ten-year age range. In the United States the **median** age is 38, in the United Kingdom it is 40, in Italy it is 45, and in Japan it is 47. Contrast this with youthful Saudi Arabia, where the median age is 27.

3 The high percentage of children and young people means that Saudi Arabia's education costs are high. Education is a priority for the Kingdom. A recent report showed that education receives 25% of the government's annual budget, making the country's education spending one of the highest in the world. As a result of its demographic profile, the government has been leading a university expansion program to **cope** with the large number of college-aged students moving through the school system every year.

4 This also has an impact on employment opportunities for young people. Youth unemployment could well become the Kingdom's biggest social challenge in the coming years. These days, the unemployment rate for Saudis between the ages of 16 and 29 is 29%. Unless Saudi Arabia's government can provide enough public-sector jobs, or attract more private-sector employers, more budget expenditure will be needed for unemployment benefits.

5 There is a similar challenge in terms of housing, with more demand than supply. This is a particular problem in places such as Jeddah, Saudi Arabia's second-largest city. Jeddah is on the coast, with a mountain range to the east, and outward expansion is geographically impossible. As a consequence, houses have become more expensive, and young people may be unable to buy their own homes.

6 Although Saudi Arabia faces several challenges in terms of education, employment, and housing as a result of its young population, it does not have to cope with the demands of an aging population. Because the country has relatively fewer old people than the places mentioned earlier, the costs of health care and **pensions** are lower. This will allow more funds to be **allocated** to improving the lives of young people.

> **"**
> **Youth unemployment could well become the Kingdom's biggest social challenge in the coming years**

3 TAKING NOTES ON MAIN IDEAS **Read the case study on pages 152–153, and take notes on the main ideas. How does having a younger overall population affect Saudi Arabia? Complete the flow chart with the problems and the solutions in the reading.**

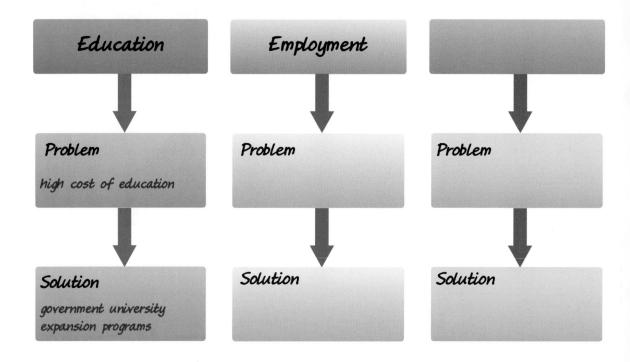

High percentage of children and young people

Education	Employment	
Problem high cost of education	**Problem**	**Problem**
Solution government university expansion programs	**Solution**	**Solution**

4 SCANNING TO FIND INFORMATION **Scan the case study. Complete each sentence with a word or number.**

1 Saudi Arabia has a very _____ population.

2 Over _____ % of the population is younger than 15.

3 Approximately _____ % of the population is between 15 and 24 years old.

4 The median age for Saudis is _____, which is 20 years younger than the median age in _____.

5 Saudi Arabia ranks as one of the top countries in the world for government spending on _____.

6 In Saudi Arabia there is a lack of employment in both the public and private _____.

7 A city that is located between the mountains and the sea has limited space for _____.

READING BETWEEN THE LINES

5 WORKING OUT MEANING **Work with a partner. Find the words and phrases in the case study and discuss what they mean.**

1 upon close analysis

2 expenditure

3 special challenges

4 as a consequence

💡 CRITICAL THINKING

6 SYNTHESIZING **Work with a partner. Use ideas from Reading 1 and Reading 2 to discuss the questions.**

APPLY	APPLY	EVALUATE
What are the advantages of a country having a younger population? What about an older population?	Does your country have more workers or retired people? Which is preferable?	Should governments raise the retirement age to reduce pension payments? Why or why not?

🗣 COLLABORATION

7 A Work in a small group. Make a list of at least three arguments for and three arguments against the following statement.

Countries with a low median age should be encouraged to emigrate and work in foreign countries with aging populations.

B Divide the class into two groups, the pros and the cons, for a class debate. Prepare an opening statement, your strongest arguments, and a closing statement.

C Have a debate. You teacher will moderate and decide the winner.

ACADEMIC COLLOCATIONS WITH PREPOSITIONS

1 Complete the phrases and phrasal verbs with the correct prepositions (*in, of, on, up, with*).

1 _____ brief

2 range _____

3 focus _____

4 sum _____

5 identify _____

6 _____ theory

7 rely _____

8 _____ contrast

2 Complete the sentences with the correct phrases and phrasal verbs from Exercise 1.

1 Countries may encounter financial challenges when an increasing number of older people have to _____ the government for support.

2 Countries with a younger population have high education costs. _____ , those with an older population have to spend more on health care.

3 There is a wide _____ voluntary work opportunities for retired people such as sports coaching, business mentoring, gardening, and counseling.

4 There is a tendency to _____ the problems faced by the elderly, not their valuable contribution to society.

5 _____ , the major problem an aging population will face is how to fund health care.

6 While many strategies may seem to work _____ , when those strategies are put into action, they rarely succeed.

7 It might be difficult for citizens of countries with aging populations to _____ the challenges of countries that have a younger population.

8 To _____ , this report's key recommendation is that more educational opportunities should be provided for people over 60.

LANGUAGE OF PREDICTION

When you describe a graph in a text, you can often predict what might happen in the future based on the trends in the graph. You can use a number of different ways to show that a statement is a prediction.

3 **Match the sentence halves.**

1	There is likely	a	be more wealthy people with more leisure time.
2	There may	b	to be more competition for places at nursing homes in the future.
3	The number of		
4	The population is set	c	projected to increase over the next several years.
5	We are unlikely to	d	to rise sharply during the next few years.
6	Unemployment is	e	young people is expected to remain the same for the foreseeable future.
7	Food prices		
		f	are predicted to come down.
		g	see a sharp rise in immigration based on current trends.

4 **Write sentences with a similar meaning. Include the word in parentheses. More than one answer is possible.**

1 The population will increase in the future. (likely)

_____

2 Oil prices will come down this year. (may)

_____

3 Unemployment will remain at the same level in the coming months. (predicted)

_____

4 The cost of living will rise over the decade. (set)

_____

5 There will be more competition for spots in colleges and universities in the future. (expected)

_____

6 There will not be a reduction in the number of schools. (unlikely)

_____

7 Salaries will rise because of access to better training and education. (projected)

_____

WATCH AND LISTEN

PREPARING TO WATCH

1   ACTIVATING YOUR KNOWLEDGE   **Work with a partner. Discuss the questions.**

1   What do elderly people you know do to keep busy?

2   How do you think everyday life has changed in the past 20 years for elderly people?

3   What are some ways elderly people stay healthy today?

2   PREDICTING CONTENT USING VISUALS   **Look at the pictures from the video. Discuss the questions.**

1   What do you think the name *Nifty after Fifty* means?

2   What activities are the elderly people in the pictures participating in?

3   Why do you think they are participating in those activities? What benefits might the activities provide?

WHILE WATCHING

3   UNDERSTANDING MAIN IDEAS   **Watch the video. Which sentence expresses the main idea?**

1   Getting older is very difficult, and some elderly people have a lot of trouble with broken bones.

2   While getting older can be a physical challenge, there are some gyms around the country that are helping the elderly stay healthy and physically fit.

3   According to research, the elderly are more physically fit because of programs that promote wellness across the country.

4 UNDERSTANDING DETAILS **Watch again. Write a supporting detail for each main idea.**

1 Nifty after Fifty is a fitness chain that offers a class with a simple goal.

_____

2 For the elderly, exercise is a weapon to prevent emergency room visits.

_____

3 Julianne Gooselaw's fitness level has changed greatly in two years.

_____

5 MAKING INFERENCES **Work with a partner. Discuss the questions and give reasons for your answers.**

1 Why do you think the exercise classes at Nifty after Fifty are so beneficial for the elderly?

2 What motivates the elderly to take classes at Nifty after Fifty?

3 What other kinds of exercise classes do you think would appeal to the elderly? Why?

☼ CRITICAL THINKING

6 **Work in a small group. Discuss the questions.**

APPLY	ANALYZE	ANALYZE
Are there programs like Nifty after Fifty in your city or country? Describe one.	What exercise classes do you, or could you, participate in now? How do you think that will change over the next 20 years?	Do you see any disadvantages to programs like Nifty after Fifty? What are they?

🗣 COLLABORATION

7 **A** Work in a small group. What other ways besides physical exercise can senior citizens stay healthy and productive? Think about:

- mental and physical health
- volunteering
- friendship and laughter
- continuing education

B Create a weekly activity program for members of a senior community center in your town or city. Present your activity program to the class.

GLOSSARY OF KEY VOCABULARY

Words that are part of the Academic Word List are noted with an (A) in this glossary.

UNIT 1 GLOBALIZATION

READING 1

authenticity (n) the quality of being real or true

discount (n) a reduction in the usual price

fresh (adj) recently made, collected, or cooked

ingredient (n) food that is used with other foods in the preparation of a particular dish

insist (v) to say firmly or demand forcefully

perfectionist (n) a person who wants everything to be perfect and demands the highest standards possible

selling point (n) a feature that persuades people to buy a product

situated (adj) in a particular place

READING 2

consumption (A) (n) the using of goods and services in an economy

convenience (n) something that is suitable to your purposes and causes no difficulty for your schedule or plans

ensure (A) (v) to make certain that something is done or happens

experiment (v) to test or to try a new way of doing something

increase (v) to become larger or greater

influence (n) the power to have an effect on people or things, or someone or something that is able to do this

relatively (adv) quite good, bad, etc. in comparison with other similar things or with what you would expect

specialty (n) a product that is unusually good in a particular place

UNIT 2 EDUCATION

READING 1

concrete (adj) based on actual things and particular examples

discipline (n) a particular area of study

evolve (A) (v) to change or develop gradually

gender gap (n) the difference in opportunities, attitudes, pay, etc. between men and women

launch (v) to begin or introduce a new plan

oriented (A) (adj) directed toward or focused on

pursue (A) (v) to try to do or achieve

underrepresented (adj) not given enough presence; in unreasonably lower numbers than others

READING 2

core principles (n phr) key values

credible alternative (n phr) reliable substitute

distance learning (n phr) general education from online instruction

modern phenomenon (n phr) recent trend

online degree (n phr) an academic qualification obtained from online instruction

significant difference (n phr) important distinction

technological advances (n phr) developments in technology

virtual classroom (n phr) online course

UNIT 3 MEDICINE

READING 1

chief (adj) most important or main

controversial Ⓐ (adj) causing disagreement or discussion

conventional Ⓐ (adj) following the usual practices

fund Ⓐ (v) to provide money to pay for something

proponent (n) a person who supports a particular idea or plan of action

substance (n) a material with particular physical characteristics

surgery (n) the cutting open of the body to repair a damaged part

symptom (n) a reaction or feeling of illness that is caused by a disease

READING 2

burden (n) a duty or responsibility that is hard to bear

consultation Ⓐ (n) a meeting with a doctor who is specially trained to give advice to you or other doctors about an illness

contribution Ⓐ (n) money, support, or other help

labor Ⓐ (n) practical work, especially work that involves physical effort

regardless (adv) despite; not being affected by something

safety net (n) something used to protect a person against possible hardship or difficulty

treatment (n) the use of drugs, exercise, etc. to improve the condition of a sick or injured person, or to cure a disease

UNIT 4 THE ENVIRONMENT

READING 1

community Ⓐ (n) the people living in one particular area

criticize (v) to express disapproval of someone or something

crucial Ⓐ (adj) extremely important or necessary

devastating (adj) causing a lot of damage or destruction

identify Ⓐ (v) to recognize something and say what that thing is

maintenance Ⓐ (n) the work needed to keep something in good condition

measure (n) a method for dealing with a situation

reduction (n) the act of making something smaller in size or amount

READING 2

casualty (n) a person hurt or killed in a serious accident or event

disrupt (v) to prevent something from continuing as expected

infrastructure Ⓐ (n) the basic systems and services, such as transportation and power, that a country uses to work effectively

issue Ⓐ (n) a subject or problem that people are thinking about or discussing

monitor Ⓐ (v) to watch and check something carefully over a period of time

policy Ⓐ (n) a set of ideas or a plan for action that a business, government, political party, or group of people follow

rely on Ⓐ (phr v) to depend on or trust someone or something

strategy Ⓐ (n) a long-range plan for achieving a goal

UNIT 5 ARCHITECTURE

READING 1

compromise (n) an agreement between two sides who have different opinions, in which each side gives up something it had wanted

conservation (n) the protection of plants, animals, and natural areas from the damaging effects of human activity

durable (adj) able to last a long time without being damaged

efficiency (n) the condition or fact of producing the results you want without waste

relevant Ⓐ (adj) related to a subject or to something happening or being discussed

secondhand (adj) not new; having been used in the past by someone else

sector Ⓐ (n) a part of society that can be separated from other parts because of its own special character

READING 2

civilized (adj) having a well-developed way of life and social systems

demonstrate Ⓐ (v) to show how to do something; to explain

depressing Ⓐ (adj) making you feel unhappy and without hope

function Ⓐ (n) a purpose, or the way something works

inspiring (adj) causing eagerness to learn or do something

reflect on (phr v) to cause people to think of someone or something in a specified way

reputation (n) the general opinion that people have about someone

UNIT 6 ENERGY

READING 1

aquatic (adj) living in, happening in, or connected with water

generate Ⓐ (v) to cause to exist; produce

inexhaustible (adj) in such large amounts that it cannot be used up

initial Ⓐ (adj) at the beginning; first

offshore (adv) away from or at a distance from the land

universal (adj) existing everywhere or involving everyone

utilize Ⓐ (v) to make use of something

READING 2

address (v) to give attention to or to deal with a matter or problem

adopt (v) to accept or begin to use something alarming (adj) causing worry or fear

diminish Ⓐ (v) to reduce or be reduced in size or importance

instigate (v) to cause an event or situation to happen

resistant (adj) not accepting of something

urgent (adj) needing immediate attention

vital (adj) necessary or extremely important for the success or continued existence of something

UNIT 7 ART AND DESIGN

READING 1

aesthetic (adj) relating to the enjoyment or study of beauty, or showing great beauty

conceptual (adj) based on ideas or principles

contemporary (adj) existing or happening now

distinction (n) a difference between similar things

established (adj) generally accepted or familiar; having a long history

notion (n) a belief or idea

significance (n) importance

READING 2

acknowledge Ⓐ (v) agree; admit something is true

analogous Ⓐ (adj) similar; comparable

banal (adj) boring; uninteresting

cynical (adj) suspicious; negative

mechanical (adj) related to machines

objective Ⓐ (adj) based on facts and reality

perceive Ⓐ (v) to think of someone or something in a particular way

sophisticated (adj) highly developed and complex

UNIT 8 AGING

READING 1

adapt Ⓐ (v) to adjust to different conditions or uses

capacity Ⓐ (n) a particular position or job; a role

demographic (adj) relating to human populations and the information collected about them such as their size, growth, ages, and education

leisure (n) the time when you are not working or doing other duties

undertake Ⓐ (v) to take responsibility for and begin doing something

voluntary Ⓐ (adj) done without being forced or paid to do it

READING 2

allocate Ⓐ (v) to give something as a share of a total amount

cope (v) deal with problems or difficulties successfully

documented Ⓐ (adj) recorded or written down

median (n) the middle number or amount in a series

pension (n) a sum of money paid regularly to a person who has retired

proportion Ⓐ (n) part or share of the whole

range Ⓐ (n) amount or number between a lower and upper limit

UNIT 1

▶ **Chinese Flavors for American Snacks**

Reporter: This Beijing supermarket's filled with brands that might look familiar but flavors that definitely aren't. Blueberry-flavored potato chips, strawberry and milk-flavored Cheetos? What about aloe juice from Minute Maid? Every major U.S. food label, it seems, is trying to bite into China's 186-billion-dollar fast-food and processed-food industries by creating new products designed just for Chinese taste buds. Tropicana cantaloupe juice, orange-flavored Chips Ahoy cookies, and Chinese herbal medicine Wrigley's Gum. But it's Frito-Lay potato chips that really push the boundaries. Early taste tests revealed that Chinese people didn't like popular American flavors like sour cream and onion. So product researchers came up with new flavors inspired by traditional Chinese food. From Sichuan spicy to sweet and sour tomato, all the way to the sugary end of the spectrum with cucumber flavor, lychee, and mango.

Harry Hui: The market is extremely competitive, so there are many new products that are being launched regularly onto the marketplace.

Reporter: Popular American chains are also getting in on the idea. McDonald's has purple taro pie. Starbucks offers coffee drinks with jelly cubes on the bottom. And KFC's got spicy squid on a stick.
These products may seem wacky in the U.S., but there's serious pressure to be the object of Chinese cravings.

Shaun Rein: China is going to become the second largest, if not largest, consumer market in the world in the next five years. So if American companies don't figure out how to get it right in China, they're going to be missing out on what should be their major generator for growth.

Reporter: Even the toothpaste companies can't afford to ignore the flavor game. From lotus flower Crest to salty Colgate. Every corner of the grocery store is trying to tempt China's curious consumers.

UNIT 2

▶ **College Debt and Bankruptcy**

Velicia Cooks: What's that one again?

Reporter: Velicia Cooks always believed a college degree would mean a better future, but at 30, faced with $80,000 in student loan debt, the future is hard to think about.

Velicia Cooks: I actually, currently, make almost exactly what I made before I had my degree.

Reporter: Today two-thirds of all students graduate in debt. The average debt is $24,000, but thousands begin their adult lives more than $100,000 in debt.

Woman: Some people say it's like graduating when you already have a mortgage, but you don't have a house.

Reporter: But the real shock comes with the repayment terms. Like many students, Cooks signed up for two kinds of loans; one federal and one private, but at the time she admits she didn't understand the distinction. Today, her $40,000 federal loan offers flexible options. Cooks pays $160 a month, but the private loan of the same amount came with very expensive, non-negotiable terms costing her $800 a month. Add the interest, Cooks will be paying $100,000—almost three times the original loan.

Woman: Private student loans are much more like a credit card or a sub-prime mortgage. They tend to have variable rates and they come with almost no consumer protections.

Reporter: For Cooks, keeping up with payments during a complicated pregnancy became too much to handle.

Velicia Cooks: To get those harassing phone calls, and it made me feel like I was a deadbeat.

Reporter: Cooks was advised to file for bankruptcy. Bad idea. Under the bankruptcy law, student loans cannot be discharged, unlike a mortgage, credit card, or even gambling debt. That education debt stays with you for life.

Felicia Cooks: It stays with you for life. I prided myself as being financially responsible.

Reporter: Cooks testified before the House Judiciary Committee to help repeal the law which prevents people from discharging private student loan debt.

Felicia Cooks: It was irresponsible on my part, wholeheartedly, for not reading the fine print. Come get me!

Reporter: For many like Cooks, that fine print will cast a big shadow for a long time.

UNIT 3

▶ A New Way to Handle Allergies

Anchor: If you forget to take your meds, doctors have come up with an easy and convenient way to make sure you get your daily dose. Marlie Hall reports.

Marlie Hall (Reporter): Derek Lacarrubba is brushing his teeth and treating his allergies at the same time.

Derek Lacarrubba: Like there's nothing about it that seems any different than an ordinary toothpaste.

Marlie Hall: The 31-year-old is allergic to dogs, cats, trees, and dust. He's one of 12 patients testing the toothpaste called Allerdent at Weill Cornell Medical College.

Dr. William Reisacher: And we have our extracts.

Marlie Hall: The toothpaste is custom-made for patients and contains extracts of what they're allergic to.

Dr. William Reisacher: So if you can contact those extracts with the lining of the mouth, then you can desensitize a patient to those allergens and essentially cure them of their allergies.

Marlie Hall: Dr. William Reisacher developed the toothpaste. He's studying whether Allerdent is more effective than weekly allergy shots or daily allergy drops.

Dr. William Reisacher: The problem is when you send a treatment home, then people forget to do it, and also it's difficult for small children to keep a liquid under their tongue for two minutes.

Marlie Hall: The toothpaste can treat up to ten different allergies at one time. There can be side effects including itching and tingling in the mouth. Lacarrubba says Allerdent has helped with his stuffy nose, and his snoring and sleep are better.

Derek Lacarrubba: I can breathe through my nose on almost all mornings.

Marlie Hall: And he can even take his dog for a walk outside and enjoy it. Marlie Hall, CBS News, New York.

UNIT 4

▶ Population and Water

Narrator: We call our Earth "the blue planet" because about 70% of the Earth's surface is covered in water. But most of that is in the oceans and seas. Just 2.5% is fresh water, and only 1% of that is available for human use. The rest is locked up in mountain passes and the Earth's polar ice caps. But there's another fact we need to understand about water.

Brian Richter: Well, there's no more water on the planet than there was when life first appeared on Earth. It changes its distribution, there's more water in different parts of the world than there were hundreds or thousands of years ago, but it's still exactly the same amount of water that's been here always.

Narrator: We use over half of all the available fresh water in the world to serve our needs: to transform deserts into fields, to produce energy from rivers, and to build cities in some of the driest regions on the planet. But despite our creativity, there are many who have difficulty getting enough of this basic resource.

Brian Richter: More than a billion people on the planet already lack access to safe, clean drinking water. And we know things are going to get more difficult as the population continues to grow. Within the next 20 years, as much as half of the world's population will live in areas of water stress.

Narrator: Many water shortages are the result of poor infrastructure, politics, poverty, or simply living in a dry part of the world. But more and more, they are due to increasing populations. Mexico City, for example, benefits from heavy annual rainfall. But its water system is stressed from supplying water to its 20 million inhabitants. The issue is the combination of leaks in the system and the fact that backup reservoirs are running dry.

In Mexico City, shops that sell water for people's daily needs are becoming more and more common. But the water we use at home is only a small percentage of the total amount of water we consume. That's because of the huge amounts used by farms and factories.

Brian Richter: We may know where the water out of our tap comes from, but we very seldom know where the water that went into our can of cola or into the shirt that we're wearing on our back, where those goods were produced and how much water it required, and what the consequences were for the natural systems in those areas and for the local communities that are dependent upon that same water. So for example, the cup of coffee that you may have in the morning requires on the order of 120 liters just to produce the coffee and bring it to your table. A can of beer 150 liters, a hamburger 8,000 liters of water, to produce enough water to grow the cotton in my shirt is 3,000 liters as well.

Narrator: The influence of humans on the world's fresh water systems is so significant that it can be seen from space. The Aral Sea, the fresh water lake in central Asia, once covered more than 25,000 square miles. But in the last 40 years, it has lost 90% of its water, with most of it going to support cotton farms. Lake Chad, on the southern side of the Sahara Desert, is now one tenth of its normal size due to drought and overuse. Yet, 30 million people still depend on it.

UNIT 5

▶ Building a Green Home

Dan Sharp: There's a lot of compost here.

Ben Tracy (Reporter): Dan Sharp decided it was time to do his part to save the planet.

Dan Sharp: A lot of things we were consuming, ways that we were living that we didn't necessarily need to be doing.

Ben Tracy: For the past five years, he's been systematically turning his century-old yellow house in Pasadena green. Dan installed solar panels on the roof, added solar tube-lighting inside, and replaced the AC with a giant house fan.

Dan Sharp: It's a little louder than a normal air conditioner, but it, you know, costs much, much less to operate.

Ben Tracy: Dan's wife, Maya, wasn't so sure about all these eco upgrades until she saw their annual electric bill.

Maya Sharp: Before it would be $1,000, $1,200 a year and now it's zero.

Ben Tracy: That type of savings has homeowners jumping on the green bandwagon. A recent survey found that 68% of those polled took steps last year to make their homes more energy efficient. Yet 71% of them said their number one reason was to save money, not necessarily the environment. Home builders struggling to find buyers in a tough market are taking note.

Man 1: This is really nice.

Ben Tracy: They're rolling out smaller, greener models, hoping to attract first-time homebuyers. What are you looking for in this sort of market?

Man 1: Cheap.

Ben Tracy: Comstock Homes is building the country's largest solar-powered community just outside Los Angeles. The sun power generated could save homeowners as much as $300 on their monthly utility bills. They think it will also spike home sales.

Man 2: By adding the solar to it, it allows us to absorb probably twice as fast the number of buyers that we normally would.

Ben Tracy: Meanwhile, Greenstreet Development, a housing startup in Phoenix, is selling green homes for as low as $115,000. They keep costs down by buying foreclosed properties and renovating them with energy-saving features. Yet one of the biggest selling points of these homes is not the savings inside, it's the savings a couple of blocks away. All of the homes are within a quarter mile of the city's new light-rail line, cutting down on commuting time and cost. Still, there's a limit on how much consumers will spend to go green.

Man 3: They're only willing to pay about 2% more than the cost of a house would normally be in order to get it green, that's a difficult balance for a builder to achieve.

Dan Sharp: In the long term, you will save money, you will definitely recoup your initial investment.

Ben Tracy: And that means Dan Sharp is seeing less of his hard-earned money washed away. Ben Tracy, CBS News, Los Angeles.

UNIT 6

▶ Wind Turbines

Daniel Sieberg (Reporter): Jerry Tuttle is a new breed of cowboy.

Jerry Tuttle: The whole desk job thing is just not for me.

Daniel Sieberg: His herd is hundreds of giant wind turbines. I climbed with Tuttle, nearly 300 feet in the air, so we could show off his penthouse office.
This is a pretty amazing workplace.

Jerry Tuttle: Well look at it, look at it, I mean that is, it is what it is, it's amazing.

Daniel Sieberg: As a turbine technician, Tuttle keeps things humming at this massive farm in Sweetwater, Texas. With 3,200 turbines, wind generates 3% of the electricity in Texas, more than any other state.

Jerry Tuttle: It's nice to know that we are, we are putting renewable energy down, and with zero pollution.

Daniel Sieberg: Companies are doing it big in Texas, but homeowners can do it small, in their own backyards.

Samuel Barr: Well, I don't screw up the environment, I save a few bucks, and it's not a bad deal.

Daniel Sieberg: In Oneida, New York, Samuel Barr's personal windmill powers everything from his cappuccino machine to his kids' computer. It cost $58,000, but the state picked up half. Last month alone, he saved over

$200 and his meter sometimes even spins backwards.

Samuel Barr: When we first put it up, I'd spend hours looking at this meter.

Daniel Sieberg: In disbelief?

Samuel Barr: Yeah, in disbelief, yeah.

Daniel Sieberg: The wind rush is on. $9 billion was invested in new wind projects last year alone—35% of alternative energy investments. But critics say it's mostly hot air.

Woman: You're building, typically building the projects way out in the middle of nowhere, long distances from the load centers.

Daniel Sieberg: Indeed, this is where the country's wind blows the most, so-called Wind Alley. But this is where the majority of people live. So getting that power to the people would mean a massive, multi-billion-dollar grid restructuring. Plus, winds die down in summer, when demand is highest. Some turbines have been known to kill migratory birds, and not everyone welcomes such a sight in their backyard.

Jerry Tuttle: When I first came to west Texas, there was this, you know, cattle, and that was it, but now you see this and the sky's the limit.

Daniel Sieberg: But even those swept up in the winds of change admit that wind will only be one piece in the alternative energy puzzle. Daniel Sieberg, CBS News, Sweetwater, Texas.

UNIT 7

▶ A Culinary Art Canvas

Reporter: A Canadian student living in London found a surprising use for the food that we normally just throw away. Lauren Purnell is her name. She uses leftovers for her art and her photography. So she turns aging fruits and vegetables into a culinary canvas. Her work is a social media success and she has more than 46,000 followers on Tumblr. We visited her in her London apartment just to watch her work.

Lauren Purnell: We're on Portobello Road, known for its great food markets and fruit stalls, which is a bit of a dream for me. So my favorite is literally the stall right outside my door. It's probably about two feet outside the front step. I think it's such an inspiring place.

Where my piece begins, um, well sometimes it begins in the fridge, especially if something's about to go off and I don't want to throw it away, then I'll, you know, use that. So for instance, today, I'm going to use some leftover tarragon that I have that's not looking particularly healthy but that's going to look fantastic, um, as a photo. I was thinking this morning about what flowers I'd want to make, um, and I decided wildflowers because they're my favorite. The other day when I was making salad, I realized that if you see the inside of the radish is a really nice white color as well. So I thought if I just took that skin off, then that would be perfect for constructing petals for my daisies so that's what I'm going to do. At this point, I think I'm going to find the middle, which I have a lemon that I used yesterday and actually am going to use the bit that's already a bit, you know, tarnished and banged up because that's going to make it look a lot more real as well.

When something's going off in the fridge and I don't want to throw it out, kind of put it there and be like, "What are you? What can we do with this?" Another really important consideration when I'm making my pieces is how the photo is going to turn out, so I tend to make all my pieces, um, either kind of early morning or late afternoon because if I get the wrong sunlight, then, you know, it won't capture the piece as it is. So I think that's probably, that's probably done, which means I get the blueberries.

UNIT 8

▶ **Senior Exercise**

Anchor: Exercise can help people of all ages, including aging seniors. Carter Evans shows us one gym that's helping older Americans find their strength.

Teacher: One, two –

Carter Evans (Reporter): This isn't your granddaughter's aerobics class.

Teacher: Three, right there and go.

Carter Evans: Call it a new twist.

Woman 1: Be careful.

Carter Evans: On an old art form. "Cane fu."

Mike Moreno: We turned the fitness equation on its head.

Carter Evans: Mike Moreno is CEO of Nifty after Fifty, a fitness chain that developed the class with a simple goal.

Mike Moreno: To actually make a senior feel powerful with something that normally represents frailty.

Berta Mayberry: Sometimes when they see you, they think, "Oh, poor thing."

Carter Evans: Berta Mayberry is 77 and anything but frail.

Berta Mayberry: I don't even walk like that. I walk like this so they know it's a weapon.

Carter Evans: The exercise itself is also a weapon, helping to prevent falls, which every year, send more than two million seniors to the emergency room. According to the Centers for Disease Control, only 35% of Americans over 65 are considered physically fit. The aches and pains take their toll, says 81-year-old Julianne Gooselaw.

Julianne Gooselaw: Five years ago, I broke my shoulder, and then I had a knee replacement a year ago.

Carter Evans: But with regular visits to the gym …

Julianne Gooselaw: Now I can do almost a mile on the treadmill, where I couldn't do that two years ago but I can now. I'm stronger now than I've ever been.

Carter Evans: It's a boon for them.

Kim Bogue: I like to fight back.

Carter Evans: Not so much for those trying to mess with them. Carter Evans, CBS News, Los Angeles.

CREDITS

The authors and publishers acknowledge the following sources of copyright material and are grateful for the permissions granted. While every effort has been made, it has not always been possible to identify the sources of all the material used, or to trace all copyright holders. If any omissions are brought to our notice, we will be happy to include the appropriate acknowledgements on reprinting.

The publisher has used its best endeavors to ensure that the URLs for external websites referred to in this book are correct and active at the time of going to press. However, the publisher has no responsibility for the websites and can make no guarantee that a site will remain live or that the content is or will remain appropriate.

Photo Credits

The publishers are grateful to the following for permission to reproduce copyright photographs and material:

Key: T = Top, C = Center, B = Below, L = Left, R = Right, TL = Top Left, TR = Top Right, BL = Below Left, BR = Below Right, CL = Center Left, CR = Center Right, BG = Background

The following images are sourced from Getty Images.

pp. 14-15: SolStock/E+; p. 16 (spot): Allison Dinner/Stockfood Creative; p. 16 (T): Yuriko Nakao/Bloomberg; p. 17: Maremagnum/Photolibrary; p. 18 (T): Ariana Lindquist/Bloomberg; p. 18 (BL): Eising/Stockfood Creative; p. 19 (TL): Leisa Tyler/Lightrocketgetty Images; pp. 18-19: Joel Carillet+E+; pp. 20-21: Westend61; pp. 22-23: Deyangeorgiev/Istock; pp. 24-25: Fcafotodigital/E+; p. 24 (C): Douglas Pearson/Stone; p. 25 (C): Gerenme/E+; p. 27: Andrew Burton; p. 29: Vladimir Zapletin/Istock; p. 30: Darrell Gulin/Photographer'S Choice; pp. 32-33: Bartosz Hadyniak/E+; p. 34: F11Photo; p. 36: Peopleimages/Digitalvision; p. 37 (TR): Monty Rakusen/Cultura; p. 37 (BR): Gary Burchell/Taxi; p. 37 (CR): Hero Images; p. 38: Buero Monaco/Corbis; p. 40: Steve Debenport/E+; p. 41: Hill Street Studios/Blend Images; p. 42: Toltemara/Istock; p. 43 (TL): Robert Daly/Caiaimage; p. 43 (TR): Blend Images - Hill Street Studios; p. 46: Peter Muller/Cultura; p. 48: Janniswerner/Istock Editorial; pp. 50-51: Fotoman-kharkov/iStock; p. 52: Nik_Merkulov/Istock; p. 53 (T): Fangxianuo/E+; p. 53 (BR): Temmuzcan/Istock; p. 54 (TL): Hemme; p. 54 (TR): Andrew Brookes/Cultura; p. 55 (TR): Science Photo Library; p. 55 (BR): Jamie Grill; p. 55 (spot): Jupiterimages/The Image Bank; p. 55 (spot): Wavebreakmedia/Istock; pp. 56-57: Cui Hao/Vcg; p. 58 (TR): Hero Images; p. 58 (TL): Paul Barton/Corbis; p. 58: Peterspiro/Istock; p. 59: Nancy Brown/The Image Bank; p. 60: Erik Mcgregor/Pacific Press/Lightrocket; p. 64: Asif Hassan/Afp; p. 66: Peterspiro/Istock; pp. 68-69: Krashkraft Vincent/Moment; p. 71 (TL): Mikhail Ter-Avanesov/Hemera; p. 71 (CL): Joe Klamar/Afp; p. 71 (BL): Andrew Holt/Photographer'S Choice; p. 71 (TR): Jiji Press/Afp; p. 71 (CR): Stocktrek Images; p. 71 (BR): Matt Cardy/Getty Images News; p. 71 (BG): Photohomepage/Istock; p. 72: Age Fotostock/Alamy Stock Photo; p. 73 (TR): Andrew Holt/Photographer'S Choice; p. 73 (BR): Victor J. Blue/Bloomberg; p. 75: Typhoonsk/Istock; pp. 78-79 (T): Xavier Zimbardo; p. 78 (BL): Bartosz Hadyniak/E+; p. 79 (TL): Martin Harvey/Corbis Documentary; p. 79 (TR): Simplycreativephotography/E+; p. 81: Danita Delimont/Gallo Images; p. 83: Kenneth Canning/E+; p. 84: Www.Infinitahighway.Com.Br/Moment; p. 85: Alexandrumagurean/Istock; pp. 86-87: Maremagnum/The Image Bank; p. 89: Kiyoshi Ota/Bloomberg; p. 90 (T): Yuji Kotani/Taxi Japan; p. 90 (BL): Christian Aslund/Lonely Planet Images; p. 91: Anna Gorin/Moment; p. 93: Ashley Cooper/Corbis Documentary; p. 94: Wendy Stone/Corbis; p. 95 (BL): Cameron Spencer; p. 95 (BC): Derek Croucher/Photographer'S Choice; p. 95 (BR): B.S.P.I./Corbis Documentary; p. 96 (T): Tonytaylorstock/Istock Editorial; p. 96 (BL): Barry Winiker/Photolibrary; p. 97 (TR): Rick Gerharter/Lonely Planet Images; p. 97 (BL): Carol M. Highsmith/Buyenlarge; p. 99: John Freeman/Lonely Planet Images; p. 101: Jon Arnold/Awl Images; p. 102: Bestgreenscreen/Istock; pp. 104-105: Danny Hu/Moment; p. 106 (1): John Harper/Photodisc; p. 106 (2): Universal Images Group; p. 106 (3): Nenov/Moment; p. 106 (4): Fred Tanneau/Afp; p. 106 (5): Banksphotos/E+; pp. 106-107: Pedrosala/Istock; pp. 108-109: Michael Betts/Digitalvision; p. 109 (B): Arctic-Images/Stone; p. 111: Manachai/Moment; pp. 112-113: Kendallrittenour/Istock; p. 114: Serenethos/Istock Editorial; p. 115: David Sailors/Corbis Documentary; pp. 116-117: Fred Dufour/Afp; pp. 118-119: Moirenc Camille/Hemis.Fr; p. 120: Paul Knightly/Istock; pp. 122-123: CliqueImages/DigitalVision; p. 124: Jean-Pierre Lescourret/Lonely Planet Images; p. 125 (a): Jeff J Mitchell/Getty Images News; p. 125 (b): Robert Alexander/Archive Photos; p. 125 (c): José Fuste Raga/Age Fotostock; p. 125 (d): Niccolo Guasti/Getty Images Entertainment; p. 126: Rudi Von Briel/Photolibrary; p. 127 (TR): Stephan Kaps/Eyeem; p. 127 (BR): Visual China Group; p. 129: Dave Etheridge-Barnes/Getty Images News; pp. 130-131: Cr Shelare/Moment; pp. 132-133: Paul Mansfield Photography/Moment; p. 133: Francois Guillot/Afp; p. 137: De Agostini Picture Library; p. 138: Redstallion/Istock; p. 139: Venturelli/Wireimage; pp. 140-141: AleksandarNakic/iStock; p. 142 (BR): Mbbirdy/E+; p. 142 (BL): Squaredpixels/Istock; p. 143: Mikolette/E+; p. 144: Westend61; p. 145 (1): Hero Images; p. 145 (2): Johner Images; p. 145 (3): Ryanjlane/E+; p. 145 (4): Tom Grill/Jgi; p. 146: Kazuko Kimizuka/DigitalVision; p. 148: Celia Peterson/Arabianeye; p. 150 (BL): Kirklandphotos/The Image Bank; pp. 150-151: Tariq_M_1/Room; p. 151 (TR): Celia Peterson/Arabianeye; p. 151 (CR): Daryl Visscher/Arabianeye; p. 153: Zouzou1/Istock; p. 154: David Jakle/Image Source; p. 156: Thinair28/Vetta.

Illustrations

by Martin Sanders (Beehive Illustration): p. 89

Video Supplied by BBC Worldwide Learning.

Video Stills Supplied by BBC Worldwide Learning.

Corpus

Development of this publication has made use of the Cambridge English Corpus (CEC). The CEC is a multi-billion word computer database of contemporary spoken and written English. It includes British English, American English, and other varieties of English. It also includes the Cambridge Learner Corpus, developed in collaboration with the University of Cambridge ESOL Examinations. Cambridge University Press has built up the CEC to provide evidence about language use that helps produce better language teaching materials.

Cambridge Dictionaries

Cambridge dictionaries are the world's most widely used dictionaries for learners of English. The dictionaries are available in print and online at dictionary.cambridge.org. Copyright © Cambridge University Press, reproduced with permission.

Typeset by QBS

Audio by John Marshall Media.

Classroom teachers shaped everything about *Prism*. The topics. The exercises. The critical thinking skills. Everything. We are confident that *Prism* will help your students succeed in college because teachers just like you helped guide the creation of this series.

Prism Advisory Panel

The members of the *Prism* Advisory Panel provided inspiration, ideas, and feedback on many aspects of the series. *Prism* is stronger because of their contributions.

Gloria Munson
University of Texas, Arlington

Dinorah Sapp
University of Mississippi

Kim Oliver
Austin Community College

Christine Hagan
George Brown College/Seneca College

Wayne Gregory
Portland State University

Heidi Lieb
Bergen Community College

Julaine Rosner
Mission College

Stephanie Kasuboski
Cuyahoga Community College

GLOBAL INPUT

Teachers from more than 500 institutions all over the world provided valuable input through:
- Surveys
- Focus Groups
- Reviews